POWER
to
Change

Top Experts Share Their Powerful Secrets

THRIVE
PUBLISHING™

THRIVE Publishing
A Division of PowerDynamics Publishing, Inc.
San Francisco, California
www.thrivebooks.com

©2011, THRIVE Publishing
All rights reserved

ISBN: 978-0-9836395-7-2

Library of Congress Control Number: 2011938783

Printed in the United States of America on acid-free paper.

URL Disclaimer
All Internet addresses provided in this book were valid at press time.
However, due to the dynamic nature of the Internet, some addresses
may have changed or sites may have changed or ceased to exist since
publication. While the co-authors and publisher regret any inconvenience
this may cause readers, no responsibility for any such changes can be
accepted by either the co-authors or the publisher.

$\mathcal{D}$edication

We dedicate this book to you, our readers,
who recognize the importance of living
a powerful and masterful life. We know
that you are ready to take steps to create
positive change in your world—and we
celebrate your commitment to being
the best, most amazing creation you can be,
for the enrichment of all!

The Co-Authors of *Power to Change*

$\mathcal{T}$able of Contents

Disclaimer

The *Power to Change* book, website and tele-class are not intended to diagnose or prescribe any treatment for any medical or psychological condition(s), nor are there any claims or offers to prevent, diagnose, treat, mitigate or cure any medical or psychological conditions. The material is for informational purposes only.

The book, website and tele-class contain the ideas and opinions of its co-authors and are intended solely to provide helpful information on a variety of subjects. It is offered with the understanding that the co-authors and publisher are not engaged in rendering medical, health or any other kind of personal professional services in the book.

As each individual situation is unique, you should use proper discretion in consultation with your medical, health or other competent professional before adopting any of the suggestions in the book.

The co-authors and publisher expressly disclaim all responsibility for any adverse effects, liability, loss, or risk, personal or otherwise, that is incurred or may result as a consequence (directly or indirectly) of the use and application of any of the information in the book, website and tele-class.

Acknowledgements

Gratitude is a key component in living a life of powerful transformation and success. Before we share our wisdom and experience with you, we have a few people to thank for turning our vision for this book into a reality.

This book is the brilliant concept of Caterina Rando, the founder of Thrive Publishing and a respected business strategist, with whom many of us have worked to grow our businesses. Working closely with many self-development professionals, Caterina realized how valuable the knowledge they possessed would be to those wanting to manifest powerful change and transformation in their lives. The result was putting these ideas into a comprehensive book.

Without Caterina's "take-action" spirit, her positive attitude and her commitment to excellence, you would not be reading this book, of which we are all so proud.

Additionally, all of our efforts were supported by a truly dedicated team, who worked diligently to put together the best possible book for you. We are truly grateful for everyone's stellar contribution.

To Ruth Schwartz, with her many years of experience and wisdom, who served as an ongoing guide throughout the project, your support to our production team and to all of the co-authors is deeply appreciated.

To Patricia Haddock, whose expertise and refined skills as an editor proved very valuable and whose magic pen ensured that this book would be the best it could be, we thank you.

To Erin Delaney, who served as project manager and copyeditor, we appreciate your encouraging spirit, positive perspective and patient guidance with our work, and we are truly grateful.

To Tammy Tribble, Tricia Principe and Barbara McDonald, our designers extraordinaire, who brought their creative brilliance to the book cover, layout and website, thank you for your enthusiasm, problem solving and attention to detail throughout this project.

To Tony Lloyd, who provided us with a keen eye and an elegant touch as a proofreader, thank you for your support and contribution for making us read so perfectly on paper.

We also acknowledge each other for delivering outstanding information, guidance and advice. Through our work in this book and with our clients and patients, we are truly committed to profoundly enhancing the lives of others. We are grateful that we get to do work that we love and contribute to so many in the process. We do not take our good fortune lightly. We are clear in our mission—to make a genuine contribution to you, the reader. Thank you for granting us this extraordinary opportunity.

The Co-Authors of *Power to Change*

Introduction

Congratulations! You have opened an incredible resource, packed with brilliant and life-changing ideas that will enhance your life in ways you cannot yet imagine. You are about to discover the magic behind the power to change.

Your personal and professional success in life comes as the result of more than talent, commitment and hard work. Your success is also determined by your own self-awareness, the systems you have in place to support you and how willing you are to embrace change within and around you. We know you want to be the absolute best you can be, and we are here to inspire, encourage and support you on your journey!

You have probably seen how even small changes in perspective and behavior can transform and uplift your life. In the following pages, you will learn how to:

- Use intentions, journaling and healthy life choices to unleash your own, great power within.

- Manage your stress and work with painful experiences from the past, so you can step into your higher purpose.

- Change your limiting beliefs into beliefs of empowerment and courage that lead to immense success.

All of the professionals you will meet in this book want you to live your most incredible life. We have outlined for you our top tips and included the most expert advice on how to bring forth potent change in your life.

To get the most out of this book, we recommend that you read it once, cover to cover. Then go back and follow the steps that apply to you in the chapters most relevant to your current situation. Every change you make will get you closer to the life you want and deserve.

Know that just learning what to do will not transform your life. You must take action and apply the strategies, tips and tactics we share in these pages to reap their many rewards. With our knowledge and your actions, we are confident that, like our thousands of satisfied clients, you too will master the *Power to Change*.

To your unlimited success!

The Co-Authors of *Power to Change*

Embracing Change
By Pat Gayman, DC

One thing I know about change is that change happens. In fact, it is the only thing we can count on with any amount of certainty. With this being the case, it makes sense to discover how to embrace change as a natural part of life. You can learn the skills and techniques of not only adapting to changes that occur from external sources, but of consciously choosing to make change happen—and make it happen successfully. You can be, do or have more in your life when you develop sustainable strategies for success, and this comes from embracing change.

Change naturally elicits fear as you move out of the familiar into the unfamiliar. This fear is normal, even when you are making a change to move toward something you desire. What is also true about change is that it can create chaos. This, too, is natural and a part of the territory. This chapter contains some ideas and strategies that will help you embrace change with greater ease and move through the chaos with less resistance.

"The need for change bulldozed a road down the center of my mind."
—Maya Angelou, African-American poet,
author and civil-rights activist

External and Internal Changes

There are some changes over which we have no control—the change of the seasons, natural disasters, national economic fluctuations and political shifts. Often, change is thrust upon us from outside events like the death of a loved one, a change in a job or a significant change in our financial situation. Learning to embrace the changes brought about by these external events may challenge you. However, you can also use them for your own personal growth.

Then, there are other major changes in life, like marriage or divorce, having a baby, going to college or buying a house. Though these may seem like external changes only, the fact is that they usually come about from internal decisions, so, ultimately, you *do* have a say about them.

There are also changes that you clearly and consciously make. For example, you may aspire to be a championship athlete, an acclaimed performing artist or a successful financial planner helping to make a difference in the lives of others. You may choose to be a loving   parent who helps shape people who will lead the world with high moral integrity. You may desire to be the best scrapbooker in the neighborhood. You may want to run the Boston Marathon®, write a best-selling book or drop a few pounds. No matter what is happening in your life and what you are striving for, it is good to know the difference between what you do have control over and what you do not.

Moving through Fear

Moving through the emotions of change takes strong commitment, clarity, passion and the determination to learn new habits. Anthony Robbins, American author and motivational speaker, coined the phrase, "constant and never ending improvement," also known as CANI. It is the way of life for those who live life with intention, purpose and joy. Yet, the very idea of making the kind of changes that help us grow and improve brings up two dominant emotions— excitement followed by fear.

Fear can roar like a lion causing sweaty palms, racing heart, elevated blood pressure, muscle tightness or a knot in the pit of your stomach. It can also be a more elusive emotion that hides itself in procrastination, busyness and beliefs that come from some old mental programming, such as, "I don't know enough," "What makes me think I can do that?" or "I'm not good enough to experience the success I desire." You may fear that you will fail, or you may actually fear success! There may be underlying thoughts that failure to achieve your desires may be more comfortable than the unknown world that success might bring.

Recognize that fear is a natural part of choosing to make a change. It will arise in some form or another, whether you want it to or not, but it is always your choice whether you choose to let it immobilize you, or you make a decision to forge ahead.

Choosing Change

In order to choose the change that is needed to forge ahead with your desires, it is helpful to examine what is most important to you.

What are your true values? The first step in choosing change is to examine your core values. This may be a difficult task for some. You may have been raised in an environment where values were *inherited* but not discussed or defined. You may have adopted values from the media, friends, religion or your work environment without giving them much conscious thought. Identifying *your* own values will give you a clear framework upon which to build the life of your dreams. Go beyond the usual items like integrity, honesty and generosity to delve into your core values about money, success, beauty and all the areas of a fulfilled life.

When you choose to *embody* your values, you will soon begin to notice whether you are making a choice that supports you or a choice that is made out of habitual self-sabotage. Now, it becomes much easier to determine how you want to show up in life—what you want to do and what you want to have. A question you might ask yourself to gain clarity is, "What legacy do I want to leave?"

What is your vision of the future? With clarity about your core values, it is time to create a compelling vision of your future. Let your imagination soar. Dream big and bold in beautiful, vibrant, living color! Embrace the possibilities that lie before you. Let your mind run wild. Get passionate. Use all your senses to paint the pictures that most align to your values and that will create the future you truly want.

What thoughts do you need to change? To bring this glorious vision, based on your values, into manifestation, you will likely need to change the behaviors and habits that have kept you from living your dreams. To get to the root of these, you need to turn to your thoughts. Habits are formed by behaviors, and behaviors are determined by thoughts.

The National Science Foundation has estimated that the average thinking adult processes approximately 50,000 thoughts every day. We are only aware of a tiny percentage of them unless we deliberately set out to take control of them. You can choose thoughts that are supportive rather than old sabotaging thoughts. Make up your mind to become more conscious of your thoughts. When you come across a thought that brings you down, change it. Begin right now to choose the positive, supportive and kind ones.

One of my favorite stories that I once heard in a lecture illustrates this point very well. A wise Native American elder was asked how he dealt with his own inner struggles. The elder replied, "It is as if I have two dogs inside of me. One of them is a really good, gentle and loving dog. The other is mean and evil and is always fighting with the good dog." When asked which one wins, he replied, "The one I feed the most."

Choose which thought you want to feed. A change in your behavior will follow the choice you make and that will lead to new habits. In the next section, you will learn some techniques for becoming more aware of your thoughts and how to take charge of them.

> *"The mind is everything. What you think you become."*
> —Buddha, Hindu Prince Siddhartha, the founder of Buddhism

Neuroscience Shows the Way

Throughout history, philosophers have asserted that a person's dominant thoughts determine the quality of their life. In recent years, neuroscientists have come to better understand how the mind affects the brain. First, let's consider the distinction between mind and brain.

Mind equals the thoughts you consciously choose and the thoughts that have literally been hard-wired into your brain by programming that was instilled from the earliest moments of conception. Thoughts are used to process daily activities and emotions. They create an intricate system of pathways in the brain that is both protective and inhibiting.

As a child, you may have been taught in a way that included values and skills to help you grow and flourish. If so, your mind likely developed the belief you were good enough and smart enough to make any change necessary. On the other hand, you may have learned to be frightened of venturing out of your comfort zone because you were taught, "the world is a dangerous place." In this case, your mind is likely not supportive or encouraging when change is at hand.

Often, people hold on to programming that was useful at the time it was instilled, but it no longer serves their adult self. For example, you were no doubt taught never to go into the street because it is very dangerous. As you matured, you replaced the thought of never going into the street with appropriate street crossing behavior. It is still dangerous, but now you know how to maneuver street crossing so you remain safe. How many areas of your life might you be stuck with a similar "it's-too-dangerous" thought? The good news is you *can* change your mind!

"We can think of things like happiness and compassion as skills that are no different from learning to play a musical instrument or tennis . . . it is possible to train our brains to be happy."
—Richard Davidson, PhD, American neuroscientist

The brain is the organ of the body that reacts to the thinking mind, to the environment, both internal and external, and to emotions. The brain is composed of various areas, each of which has a different function. For the sake of understanding, we will consider only two of these areas. One is the *amygdala,* which is the seat of the emotions. The other is the *frontal lobe,* which is the part of the brain that decides on action, regulates behavior, plans the future and is responsible for firm intention.

Every thought the mind creates or remembers is processed through a series of filters that set off a cascade of chemical changes in the brain and in the body. As those changes occur, heightened levels of awareness allow you to choose whether your thinking is supportive or is sabotaging you. At the moment that a different thought is chosen, a shift in your brain and your body's chemistry takes place.

People sometimes resist change based on old thinking like, "That's just the way I am," or "My whole family is like this, so it must be genetic." In Bruce H. Lipton's book, *The Biology of Belief,* published in 2005 by Hay House, he explains that changing limiting thoughts to positive, supportive, healthy thoughts can change cellular reactions and biochemical reactions.

The value of understanding how change occurs in the brain reinforces the idea that no matter how big, onerous, exciting or challenging a change may be, you can use the tools of the mind to activate the power of the brain. Sophisticated technology has allowed observation of the changes that take place during periods of focused attention on a new or repetitive thought. The frontal lobe literally lights up, and like a spark, sets the brain and body into motion. This is how change occurs.

Change Your Mind: Tools for Sustainable Success

There are many ways to encourage the mind to change, so you can consciously reprogram the hard wiring in your brain to have more supportive thoughts. Systems such as self-hypnosis, biofeedback, purposeful meditation, Pysch-K®, NET® or Neural Emotional Technique and many others are available.

Emotional Freedom Technique®, or EFT as it is known, is one of the most effective and easiest ways I have found to create a change of mind. It is an energy healing system that combines the tenets of psychology with traditional oriental understanding of how energy flows in the body. EFT uses acupressure points and meridians to stimulate the emotional response area of the brain to release the stress of emotional trauma being held in the body. This system is easy to learn and can be quickly used to help you release old habits and programs you may be holding onto. You can readily learn this technique on your own by searching the Internet or you can connect with a practitioner. Once you have cleared some of your emotional baggage, you will find it is much easier to create the intense focus that activates your brain and brings about the changes you desire.

"The world we have created is a product of our thinking;
it cannot be changed without changing our thinking."
—Albert Einstein, German physicist

Additional Tips for Change

Changing your mind takes time, determination and diligence. Here are some additional tips that can help sustain you as you navigate your way through your journey of embracing change.

Record your thoughts. Get a journal or a simple spiral notebook and write down your thoughts, feelings, fears, victories, dreams and beliefs. Doing this can help you sort out your life and discover what is most important and valuable to you. If you do not like to write, then get a small tape recorder and speak about what is on your mind. You can speak or write about the dreams you have for your life or make note of the things you are grateful for every day. (For more information on journaling, see Janet Wiszowaty's chapter, "Journaling at the Heart of Changing Your Life" on page 133).

Meditate. There is no one right or wrong way to meditate. What is most important is to sit silently and pay attention to your breath. Allow time for the incessant mind chatter to die down. You can listen to soothing music if it helps you. Whether it is for five minutes or twenty minutes, any time you quiet your mind, you come closer to hearing your own inner wisdom.

Visualize. Visualize what your life will be like when you make the changes you desire to make. See all the details of what you want. Do this before you go to sleep at night and just as you are waking up in the morning. An additional step you can take is to create a *vision board* using pictures or words from magazines to depict what you want to bring into your life.

Repeat affirmations. Create positive phrases that support your highest well-being. For example, *I am powerful. I take actions towards my dreams every day.* You can write your affirmations on Post-its® and put them everywhere, like in your sock drawer, on the front of your computer, inside a cabinet you frequently use, on the dash of your car, on the wallpaper of your phone and so on. Repeat them every time you see them.

Keep good company. Spend time with people who make you feel good about yourself. Make sure they know how to embrace change and can easily support and encourage you to grow and change in beneficial ways.

Put your body in motion. There are many ways to move your body, including dance, *tai chi* or yoga. You can take a walk in nature or a swim in the ocean. You can do these activities alone or with others. Whatever you do, enjoy being alive in your body!

Whether you are currently dealing with a change brought on by external forces, or you have made up your mind to change your life in a way that will help you step up to a new level, you now have ideas and tools to help you embrace change. As you have learned, you do indeed have the power to change once you make up your mind!

PAT GAYMAN, DC
Life Skills and Business Coach

(916) 409-9227
drpat@capacitycoach.com
www.capacitycoach.com

E mbracing change describes Pat's life. She was raised as a military child who was taught to make the best of circumstances no matter where she landed. It is her belief that everyone has an untapped capacity to do or be whatever he or she can dream. She helps people develop clarity about how they want to live and the passion to put their fears aside to claim their best life. She is a master at asking the right questions.

Pat's vast experience includes raising seven children while owning and running a highly successful multi-discipline health care facility. Next, she was a professor at a chiropractic college while also being the administrator of an active outpatient clinic. Her current business, Capacity Coach, was started in 1998. Pat was named Businesswoman of the Year by the Redding Chamber of Commerce and has received numerous other business and professional awards.

Pat regularly writes an e-newsletter entitled *Attitude Adjustments*. She is also a co-author in a book about living a life of service. As a lively, informative and entertaining speaker, she has encouraged and trained audiences worldwide for more than twenty-five years.

CPR for Your Soul
Breathing Life into Change
By Beverly Lenz, RN, MS

When you think of making a change, what do you feel? Dread? Fear? Excitement? All of the above? How you feel about change depends on many factors—the nature of the change, whether you view it as positive or negative and how much of an impact it will have on your life. Surprisingly, many people feel fear around any change—positive or negative! For example, you might be excited about getting married and, at the same time, fear the lifestyle changes this marriage will bring about. You may be eager to take a new job and also fearful about failing. You want a baby, yet are terrified of the responsibilities of parenthood.

When a change is positive, why would you feel negative emotions around it? This does not seem to make sense. It is not logical—and this is the whole point. Change is not logical. At its heart, change is emotional—it exposes your beliefs around your ability to handle the change. Using my innovative program, *CPR for Your Soul,* I have helped hundreds of people easily and quickly turn negative emotions around change into positive ones. In this chapter, I am going to give you tools and pointers you can use on your own to tap into this powerful source of freedom from fear and worry and release some self-sabotaging beliefs around change.

The Secret Behind *The Secret*

Renewed interest in the age-old concept of The Law of Attraction catapulted into mainstream, popular culture by the book *The Secret* by Rhonda Byrnes, published by Simon and Schuster in 2006. These processes simply state that what you think about, you bring about. If you keep thinking about debt, failure and ill health, you get more of it. By the same token, when you focus and act on abundance, wealth and health, these become yours. However, most people do not know how to focus on something without fear or worry. Many believe that they have to worry or something bad will happen. Then, when or if they get what they want, they fear it will be taken away just as quickly—perhaps because they believe that they do not deserve success or that happiness never lasts.

You can recite positive affirmations all day, use will power until your brain feels like it will explode and look for the kernel of positivity in everything and not make change any easier, leaving you more frustrated and depressed. Affirmations, will power and positive thinking are not enough. However, you can stop negativity and self-doubt and produce the positive changes you want in your life now by utilizing these two secrets behind "the secret."

1. Change your limiting beliefs at the cellular level. A limiting belief like, "If I am successful, I will be alone" may prevent you from realizing success since the physical signs of success might leave you open to judgment, jealousy and feelings of being unloved—giving new meaning to "it's lonely at the top." Being alone is a primitive fear for most people, dating from prehistoric times when it was dangerous to be without your tribe. A part of your mind senses a threat to your survival and sabotages you to keep you safe and alive. Not exactly what you want. Changing self-sabotaging beliefs allows you to move forward more easily and quickly.

2. Change your emotions from negative to positive. Imagine you repeatedly use the affirmation, "I am rich" and focus on being rich. When you look in your wallet, you realize you are broke and cannot even afford lunch. This creates doubt and fear of poverty—certainly not a vibrational match to wealth! However, if you focus on the affirmation of "I am in the process of becoming rich," your emotion changes to hope and positive expectation.

The real secret to creating what you want in your life is changing self-sabotaging beliefs to empowering ones at the cellular level and staying as often as possible in the "feel-good feeling." It is not only what you think about, it is what you *believe* about what you think and what you *feel* about it that manifest your desires.

You Are of Two Minds

Your mind possesses two distinct, interdependent and characteristic parts—the conscious and subconscious mind. Think of the subconscious mind as being the hard drive of your computer, storing data like past memories and experiences. According to cellular biologist Bruce H. Lipton in his book *The Biology of Belief,* published by Hay House in 2005, every cell in the body is like a programmable computer chip. The subconscious mind tells the cells what to do—"digest your dinner and keep your heart beating," for example. It also programs the cells with "tapes" derived from perceptions of events and situations. If you have ever said, "My mate knows how to push my buttons," you have reacted to a stimulus-response tape of a behavior stored at the subconscious level. Lipton says that ninety-five percent of our behavior is subconscious.

The job description of your subconscious is to keep you safe and alive. If you have experienced a traumatic change, especially at an early age, that did not work out well from the perception of the subconscious, you may have belief systems around change that do not serve you now. These subconscious beliefs could have occurred around any change the subconscious perceived as *bad*. We often blame ourselves for not being good enough and for occurrences such as parental divorce, birth of a sibling, relocation and so on.

The conscious mind, on the other hand, chooses and sets goals. It is the "I" in the equation. *I want to skydive. I want to be an opera singer. I want to finish this project.* However, any trauma stored in the subconscious may prevent you from taking action. The trauma of having fallen out of a tree when you were ten may stop you from skydiving. A parent's voice telling you that you would never amount to anything keeps you from becoming an opera singer. A public reprimand from a teacher about a mistake on the blackboard may stop you from finishing projects. You draw people and events to you based on your belief systems. These beliefs function like computer programs in the hard drive of your subconscious, creating sickness or health, wealth or poverty, happiness or unhappiness, love or loneliness. They also form your perceptions of yourself, such as powerful or powerless, fearful or safe, trusting or suspicious, worthy or worthless.

No matter how much your conscious mind wants to do something, subconscious beliefs can keep you trapped in old patterns and behaviors. By accessing your own subconscious mind, you can free yourself from old scripts that undermine your self-confidence, your physical health, interpersonal relationships and prosperity. Your subconscious mind blocks you from making those needed changes to move forward.

The Language of Energy—Good or Bad Vibes

Our universe and everything in it is made of energy, including your body, mind, thoughts, beliefs and feelings. Energy is present at all times and in all places and is in constant motion. Your focus and concentration increase the vibration of energy. Therefore, if you hold on to negative emotions, such as fear, anger, guilt, grief, unworthiness and so on, you are disallowing the fulfillment of your desire. In the book *Ask and It Is Given* by Esther and Jerry Hicks, published by Hay House in 2005, the authors write, "Our emotions are absolute indicators of what we are attracting." You need cutting-edge techniques to help you get and stay happier and healthier, move through change with grace and ease and live the life you desire.

First Aid to Survive Change

Whether it is a sudden, life-altering change or a much-desired change, it can create fear of the unknown and a paralyzing sense of loss of control. Having a strategy and changing your thoughts, feelings and beliefs put you back in control. Here are some important tools for surviving planned and sudden change.

- Fake it until you make it. Pretend you have the skills and confidence you need until you have them.

- Encourage yourself like a baby learning to walk. The words, "You can do this," and "Take one step at a time" provide a confidence boost even when they are coming from your own mouth.

- Engage in an activity daily that you can completely control. For example, train for a marathon or start practicing yoga daily.

- Accept what is and put your focus on where you want to be. View where you are now as a beginning and ask yourself, "Where do I want to be six months from now?"

- What would you tell a friend to do in a similar situation? Take the same advice.

- Celebrate small successes. Achieve wins by setting a doable goal each day. For example, a man starting a new business can make three calls each day to prospective clients.

- Put your focus on the solution rather than the problem. Most think about problems more than the tools they have for overcoming them.

Change Limiting Beliefs

Now, let's change some limiting beliefs that may keep you paralyzed by wanted and unwanted change. First, read through the entire process following this introduction.

1. Begin by sitting comfortably and placing your hand on your heart. As you do so, put your attention on your heart.

2. Take a deep breath and as you exhale, center your breath into your heart. Inhale and exhale several times as you breathe into your heart, feeling relaxed.

3. Say the following statement, "These teachings are energetically downloaded and saved into every cell of my body."

4. Read the statements below, one at a time. At the end of each statement say, "Yes!" aloud or silently, then take a deep breath into your heart and feel the energy flow throughout your body.

- I would like to know the highest perspective on the process of change.

- I would like to know how to deal with expected change and unexpected change with grace and ease.

- I would like to know how to stay in the moment and still take positive steps forward.

- I would like to know what it feels like to flow with change and know I am safe.

- I would like to know how to let go of the old and welcome the new easily.

- I would like to know the difference between being comfortable and being stuck from the highest perspective.

- I would like to know how to become unstuck without becoming unglued.

- I would like to know how to breathe with relaxation through change.

- I would like to know how to see promise and joy through the change and in the future.

- I would like to know how to have "control" through the change by being in control of my thoughts and the way I think and feel about things.

Remember to say "Yes" at the end of each statement. By saying yes, you become a co-creator in these belief changes, and you give them more power and depth. You program your beliefs to change at the subconscious level by accessing your cells' own Divine Intelligence. When you finish this process, notice what is different in the coming week about how you view change and what is different in other areas of your life. Occasionally, the subconscious has a benefit in not changing a specific belief, so if nothing changes, ask yourself what the benefit is of not changing.

I work with clients to help them release negative feelings and beliefs using a similar process. I encourage you to try this for yourself for immediate relief.

> *"When you change the way you look at things,*
> *the things you look at change."*
> —Wayne Dyer, American author and speaker

Breathing Life into Change

In 2001, before I started my business, I was diagnosed with breast cancer. I was paralyzed by an unexpected change and overwhelmed by my feelings. I probably went through all the stages of grief and loss all day, every day! My natural response was to suppress my feelings in order to be strong. I knew that resisting my feelings would only hinder my healing, so I set a timer for fifteen minutes a day to allow all my feelings free reign—to really wallow in them—for the first time in my life. After the fifteen minutes, I imagined gathering them up and putting them outside myself until the next day in which I would set the timer, bring them down and start feeling them all over again.

I found by giving myself permission to feel my feelings every day for a set amount of time, I was not paralyzed by them and could easily control my thoughts and feelings until the next day, bringing me peace. After a week or so of this, I felt rather bored with it and realized I could feel the feelings as they came up and then let them go. I began feeling peace and joy in the moment as my days unfolded.

Whenever you perceive an experience as a setback, whether it is a fight with a friend, a leaky faucet or a root canal, you generate powerful emotions that create stress in your cells. Have you ever seen two geese squabble? They go at each other furiously and then fly off flapping their wings to dispel the negative energy. What is the difference between you and the geese? You have a tendency to hold on to negative emotions that create stress in your cells. You can even take on other people's negative energy that can change or intensify your own feelings.

There is a way for you to change your feelings instantly from negative to positive through emotional acupressure points on your body and bring an instant lift to your mood and your life. Through the following process, you can release energy that you no longer want and return to feel-good feelings that attract what you want to create in your life.

Again, read the following instructions first and then take each step in order.

1. Begin by sitting comfortably and place your hand and your attention on your heart.

2. Take a few deep breaths and exhale into your heart until you feel yourself relaxing.

3. Begin thinking about making the change you would like to see in your life and intend it is so.

4. Keeping your hand on your heart, place your other hand on your abdomen and say, either aloud or to yourself, "I let go, expect the best and embrace change."

5. Take a deep breath and feel the energy of your breath move into those points on your body.

6. Now, place one hand on your throat and one hand on your forehead and say, "I am worthy of safe and peaceful change."

7. Take a deep breath and feel the energy of your breath move into these points on your body as you visualize making your change with grace and ease and intending it is so.

Notice how you are feeling. Most people feel lighter. Then, after a few moments, they experience a shift in the intensity of their feelings. This is an excerpt from the process I call *CPR for Your Soul.* You can return to this process whenever you are feeling fear, lack of confidence or negative emotion around change. Remember, this particular process only changes the intensity of emotions, not beliefs.

The processes in this chapter have given you the tools to release some limiting beliefs around change and to change them into positive ones. After utilizing these processes, take note of what is different in your life—be grateful for the change and the positive energy of gratitude will allow more good things to come. By putting these tools and techniques into practice, you can harness the power of change and transform your life.

BEVERLY LENZ, RN, MS

Discover the missing peace in your life

(760) 345-0347
beverly@beliefchangesystems.com
www.beliefchangesystems.com

Since 2003, Beverly has been developing and using belief change techniques, which have led her to formulate Belief Change Systems.™ Utilizing her own unique, cutting edge methods, she has become a transformational expert by helping others master their mindset at a cellular level quickly and easily and revealing their potential in business and life. She helps guide her clients back home to their truest, highest, deepest self.

Beverly teaches her life-changing methods through seminars and workshops and is a licensed provider by the state of California for continuing education credits for medical professionals. She has extensive counseling experience, training in crisis intervention, team building, group empowerment and relationships. Her unparalleled process helps release post-traumatic stress disorder effortlessly. She has helped businesses and individuals become more productive, prosperous and empowered, as well as happier and healthier.

Her acclaimed classes, workshops and newsletters have made Beverly a sought-after speaker and mentor for individuals, groups and companies. She is at the forefront of belief change at the cellular level. This is the true mind-body connection, and it is becoming the cornerstone for the science of the millennium.

Believe in Your Greatness
Reclaim the Life You Were Designed to Live

By Alletta Bayer, LMFT, CDC, CNHAAT

In today's consumer-driven society, people are encouraged to believe that their greatness as a person is reflected in doing or acquiring those things that lead to fortune, fame or power. However, many who have achieved success in these terms ask themselves, "Is this all there is?"

The problem in striving for externally measured values by the standards of someone else is that you become disconnected from your true self, your essence, your soul. If you measure your greatness and self-worth by your latest accomplishment or acquisitions, then nothing is ever enough. No amount of riches, accomplishments or personal decorations will keep you satisfied for long.

As America's Greatness Coach™, I believe the answer to long-term happiness and lasting fulfillment starts by going within to get in touch with your personal character strengths. This is what I call your Greatness Signature™. With this foundation, you can use your strengths, talents and passions to find your ideal work, live with meaning and make abundant contributions to the world. Living in your greatness transforms not only yourself—it allows you to make a difference in the lives of others. It opens up a whole new world of possibilities and opportunities for personal and professional growth.

If you long to feel vitally alive and are ready to change, this chapter will assist you in going within to reconnect with and claim your greatness. I will offer you some exercises to build a strong foundation from which to flourish.

> *"I know for sure that what we dwell on is who we become."*
> —Oprah Winfrey, African-American
> entertainer and television producer

You Have the Power to Change

In the book *Authentic Happiness,* by psychologist Martin Seligman, published in 2002 by The Free Press, the author states that hundreds of studies since the 1980s show that about fifty percent of almost every personality trait turns out to be attributable to genetic inheritance. Some high heritability traits, like body weight, do not change much at all, while other highly heritable traits, like pessimism or fearfulness, are changeable. The good news about this is that by putting attention on your positive strengths, which I call greatness traits, you stand in your greatness. This opens you up to your optimal success.

As a young child, I remember enthusiastically singing, "This little light of mine, I'm gonna let it shine . . . " over and over again. This little song, written by Harry Dixon Loes in the 1920s, taught me I had a light inside, a unique something I was meant to share, even though at that time, I would not have been able to articulate what it was. The song gave me the confidence to speak up and to share ideas I had, even at that tender age.

I was encouraged to believe in my greatness. Countless readings by my mother of the book *The Little Engine That Could* by Watty Piper, published in 1930 by Grosset & Dunlap, taught me about the power of positive thinking. It showed me that I could do great things if I believed in myself. It awakened the qualities of optimism and perseverance. The more I practiced these qualities, the stronger they became.

If you are rolling your eyes at these simple concepts, you might be surprised to learn some of today's foremost thought leaders in the growing field of positive psychology agree that belief in your greatness and positive thinking are the keys to lasting change and happiness.

"We either make ourselves happy or miserable.
The amount of work is the same."
—Carlos Castaneda, Peruvian-born American author

Positive Psychology and Greatness

Let us start by looking at two significant developments in the areas of psychology and personal growth. In the past few years, there has been an important shift in psychologists' understanding of what gives people the power to change and live happy, fulfilling lives. In his 1998 presidential address to the American Psychological Association, Seligman urged psychologists to "turn toward understanding and building the human strengths to complement our emphasis on healing damage." With that speech, today's positive psychology movement was launched. Rather than trying to weed out weaknesses, positive psychology emphasizes capitalizing on your strengths to live a successful life.

In the 1990s, psychotherapist Howard Glasser created The Nurtured Heart Approach®, initially as a way of working with intense and difficult children. Since then, his body of work has grown to encompass all manner of relationships, from individual personal development to business relationships. His work is ultimately about manifesting greatness. In the book *You Are Oprah,* co-written by Glasser and Melissa Block, published in 2009 by Nurtured Heart Publications, Glasser defines greatness as "the splendor of living one's dreams, the bounty of living one's passion and the valor of bringing that greatness to the world." You always have a choice to stand in your greatness or succumb to your insecurities and fears—the choice is truly yours.

Both philosophies acknowledge that each day, there are numerous choices you make that create and shape your life. You are the director of your life. You choose how to interpret situations. You choose your intentions and where to put your focus.

Belief in your greatness does not deny, eradicate or ignore emotions of sadness, frustration, anger, grief, or any other of the human emotions that are not characterized as positive. Acknowledging your greatness is a way of connecting with the light of your soul, the essence of who you are. It is not about being conceited or pounding your chest. It is a self-love that gives you inner strength and reveals the secret of how you can effectively contribute your unique gifts. It is a wellspring of renewable energy from which to give abundantly without becoming depleted.

> *"Be yourself. Everyone else is already taken."*
> —Oscar Wilde, Irish author

Your Unique Greatness Signature

I am of the belief that every individual has a unique Greatness Signature. Your Greatness Signature is a combination of the positive traits that define who you are at your core. Perhaps, when you first experienced a greatness trait, you had a sense of excitement—feeling like you were in your element, so to speak. You may have felt a surge of energy when you expressed it.

I had a client who, when she was a teenager, first discovered her leadership greatness. She attended a high school that had a strict dress code most of the teens felt was too old-fashioned. The head of school overheard her expressing her views. He challenged her to break the dress code the next day by wearing pants instead of a dress or skirt. He told her if she had the courage to do that, he would update the dress code. Nervous and exhilarated, she wore pants the next day and instantly became known as a courageous leader. Finding that signature strength at an early age has served her well. From that empowering experience, she has created opportunities to excel as a leader and positively affect the lives of many.

As life unfolds, you often become aware of more of these gifts that define you. Your strong, positive qualities that started appearing as a child, those strengths that others noticed in you, even strengths that surfaced when you most needed them—these are the foundation of your greatness. You may have created projects or pursued work that allowed you to showcase your strengths. You may even feel you cannot be stopped from displaying your greatness traits.

Once you discover your Greatness Signature, you can acknowledge, nurture and develop the specific character traits that will support you to live in your greatness. I am not talking about all the traits you would *like* to have—I'm talking about the few solid traits, somewhere between two and five, that you recognize as being the "real you," when you are at your best.

The question is, "How do you find your Greatness Signature?" I invite you to do the following exercises to assist you in this process. My suggestion is to read through the directions first and then begin the process.

Step 1: Identifying Your Character Strengths

Seligman and psychologist Christopher Peterson spent three years researching character strengths and virtues that are valued and can be identified across cultures. Out of hundreds of possibilities, they identified some of the most important strengths of character, which they grouped into six categories of virtues in their book *Character Strengths and Virtues*, published by American Psychology Association in 2004.

The list below includes the strengths they identified, grouped into categories. I expanded the list to include some strengths recognized by other names, as well. For example, *kindness* has many different forms, such as generosity, nurturance and compassion, so I chose to add them to the list. Please read through the list and write down the strengths you identify with.

• **Wisdom and knowledge**–Creativity, curiosity, open-mindedness, love of learning and perspective

• **Courage**–Bravery, persistence, perseverance, integrity, authenticity, vitality and enthusiasm

• **Humanity**–Love, kindness, generosity, nurturance, compassion, social, emotional and personal intelligence

• **Justice**–Active citizenship or loyalty, fairness and leadership perspective

• **Temperance**–Forgiveness, mercy, humility, modesty, prudence, self-regulation and self-control

• **Transcendence**–Appreciation of beauty, excellence, gratitude, hope, optimism, humor, playfulness, spirituality and purpose

Step 2: Inner Journey Method

For this step, you will need to find a quiet space without any interruptions. Have some writing materials handy, or you can use your computer if you prefer. Have also the list of the character traits from the previous step nearby.

- Get in a comfortable sitting position with your feet flat on the floor. Close your eyes. Take a few deep, slow breaths to center yourself.

- Once you feel relaxed and calm, recall a time or a situation in your life when you felt your most authentic self or were at your very best. Maybe you felt extremely alive or invigorated or internally motivated to act in a certain way. Feel the feelings or see or hear the situation that pulled out this authenticity in you. Notice the details. Really feel the feeling and experience the situation.

- When you are ready, slowly open your eyes.

- Write or type the feelings or qualities that characterized you in that situation. Write as few or as many as you want.

- You can repeat this same process a couple more times, drawing on different situations where you felt authentically you and writing down any different qualities that come to you. Take special note if there are the same qualities in each situation.

Step 3: Asking Others

Inviting the observation and experience of others is an added bonus to self-exploration and understanding. For this part, you will need the assistance of those who know you well.

- Ask those to whom you are closest to tell you the qualities they most admire in you or the character strengths they feel most define who you are. Invite them to give you examples of when those qualities were apparent to them. They may name the same qualities you find in yourself already, or they may surprise you and say something totally different. Either way, honor their valuable input.

• Pull together all of the character traits you have from the three lists. Read each trait aloud to yourself and rate each one from one to five—five being that you identify with it most strongly, and one being that with which you do not resonate at all. Put your number rating next to each trait.

• Find the top few highest-rated character traits. These traits are likely your Greatness Signature.

• Write down your greatness traits and take ownership of them. For example, you can write, "I have the strengths of optimism, love of learning and perseverance." This is your Greatness Signature. Congratulations! Claim it fully!

> *"There are powers inside of you which,*
> *if you could discover and use, would make of you*
> *everything you ever dreamed or imagined you could become."*
> —Orison Swett Marden, American writer

Additional Support for Knowing Your Greatness Signature

Here are some specific questions to bring clarity to your unique Greatness Signature. I suggest you read each question through before you begin. I also recommend that you center yourself first by taking a few deep, slow breaths.

• **How would you like to be remembered?** Imagine, for a few minutes, that the future is here. You are 99 years old and have lived a long and fulfilling life. Using the past tense, write a letter to your loved ones, highlighting your strengths and how you used them to become everything you wanted to be and lived the life you always dreamed of. The letter can be as long as you like. When you are finished, re-read it. If your life is on that path now, congratulate yourself. If you need to make some adjustments, use your Greatness Signature to recreate yourself in greatness.

• **What dreams do you want to create?** Are you living your dream now? Do you have a dream you want to manifest? Are you in need of a new dream? Dreams are gifts from your soul and encourage you to grow and stretch as a person. Much more than you realize is within your reach if you put your attention on it. Incorporating your Greatness Signature into building your dream will align the integrity of who you are with the intention you have for your dream.

• **What work or purpose do you feel compelled to do?** Write down two or three things that you have felt continually drawn to throughout your life. Check your Greatness Signature to see if those things allow you to express your greatness traits. Are you on that path now, or do you need some adjustment to live fully expressing your greatness?

After finding your Greatness Signature, the next thing to assess is whether or not you are living in the integrity of your strengths. You can use your Greatness Signature to guide you in making career or personal choices. Perhaps you need to make some changes for your long-term happiness and fulfillment. For this, I encourage you to ask another for help. It is often easier for someone else to evaluate things objectively and ask you questions that lead you to discover how you can best use your strengths, talents and passion to express your greatness in the world.

I encourage you to work with a certified Nurtured Heart Approach® specialist to help you manifest your greatness. You can also hire a certified Dream Coach® if you need a new dream or want help with one you are working on. Building on your Greatness Signature, they can guide you through a very structured and effective plan to help you get your dream into action.

Now that you are aware of your personal Greatness Signature, you have a magic formula to use again and again for guidance. Nourish your strengths. Grow them, and they will serve you well. Create a life that allows you to contribute your strengths and reclaim the life you were designed to live. Commit to letting your light shine and enjoy the bounty of standing in your greatness!

ALLETTA BAYER, LMFT, CDC, CNHAAT
America's Greatness Coach™
and Speaker

Fulfill the calling of your soul!

(415) 519-9933

alletta@allettabayer.com

www.allettabayer.com

Alletta Bayer's mission is to empower leaders to ignite their fires of greatness, so they can manifest their purpose and fulfill the calling of their soul. She specializes in conducting workshops to help clients rekindle their fires of passion and create the life they are uniquely designed to live, filled with meaning, purpose and productivity. Her extensive research and study of personal performance and emotional development models enable her to provide participants with simple, structured and effective solutions to transform from burned out to energized.

Since 1992, Alletta has been committed to helping people flourish. She has a gift for understanding people and skillfully assesses their situation. Selecting the most appropriate modalities, she coaches and guides her clients to achieve optimal personal or business fulfillment.

Alletta holds a master of arts degree in clinical psychology from John F. Kennedy University, California. She is a certified Dream Coach® and Dream Coach Group Leader, certified Nurtured Heart Approach Advanced Trainer, licensed True Purpose™ Coach, graduate of the Professional Coaching Course from New Ventures West, certified clinical hypnotherapist, practitioner of Emotional Freedom Technique® and Theta Healer® and a licensed marriage and family therapist.

The Five Vital Energies of Change
What Doctors May Not Tell You
By Carol Connick, MD

When you think of the change you want, need or deserve in your life, what is your first reaction? Are you excited about it, or do you feel panic or overwhelmed—or perhaps a mixture of emotions? This is normal. Stepping into the unknown can be both thrilling and terrifying at the same time. Nevertheless, change is just a natural part of our existence that we all must face.

If you look at your life, you will see that change occurs every day. Some changes happen often, like changing your clothes. Some are infrequent, like changing your furniture. Some changes are easy, such as clicking the television channel, whereas some are difficult, like changing a flat tire. Sometimes you can accomplish the change yourself, and sometimes you need expert help. Then, there are those changes you would simply rather not do at all, like cleaning the toilet.

In medical school, I was taught to always encourage my patients to just take action—eat well, exercise, lessen your stress and take medications. However, taking action is not always easy or permanent. As we all know, wishful thinking does not usually lead to success. In this chapter, we will explore what physicians are not taught in medical school—how influences or energy in and around us affects our health, happiness, productivity and ability to change. We will examine five vital energies or influences of change. By understanding and applying these five energies, you can transform your wishful thinking and actions into empowered choices for successful results.

"Vision without action is a daydream.
Action without vision is a nightmare."
—Japanese proverb

How Do You Create the Change You Want?

What aspects have you wanted to change in your life? Your health, weight, home, job or income—even your spouse, parents or kids? Have you ever tried to change internal factors, such as your emotions, habits, attitudes or beliefs?

With more than twenty years of experience as a family physician, I have seen the difficulties and frustrations of people needing to change. I have witnessed how their lack of change causes stress, depression, pain, obesity, disease—even premature death. On the other hand, I have also witnessed others create tremendous shifts when confronted with cancer, an abusive partner, a layoff or the loss of a loved one.

What makes a person more likely to change and be successful at creating what they want? First, they accept full responsibility for where they are now. Next, they make a solid decision to change. Then, they create clear, specific goals for the change they desire. What significantly supports lasting change is understanding and utilizing the *Five Vital Energies of Change*. Mastering these energies will help you:

• Maximize your potential to change.

• Accelerate your actions with less effort.

• Increase your success and expand your results.

• Create permanent changes you desire and deserve.

• Lessen your frustration, fear, anxiety, time and effort.

A Brief Lesson in Science

Before we go into the *Five Energies of Change,* I think it is important to have a brief lesson about energy. Much of our understanding about life comes from biology, physics, chemistry and quantum physics. The human body and all living organisms are made up of cells. Simply stated, each cell contains a nucleus and other living cytoplasm. Each nucleus has DNA comprised of atoms. Each atom has subatomic particles called *quanta.* Each of these particles is energy. In summary, humans are energy.

Energies have the ability to influence and transform. Food in the form of sugar, protein and fat becomes chemical energy for our bodies. This is changed into movement or kinetic energy. Metabolism is the balance between chemical energy and kinetic energy—the excess energy is stored in our body as fat.

Natural energies include wind, water, gravity, magnetism and light. These tangible, or measurable, energies can physically affect our bodies, inside and out.

Intangible energies—those energies that are subtle to see, feel and measure—are both positive and negative and affect our physical, mental and emotional health. Every time you think a thought, neurochemicals, or chemical energy, is released. Emotions, such as anger, joy and excitement, are considered *energy in motion.* A hug transfers positive and loving energy from one person to another. A nasty glare conveys negative and repelling energy. We have all experienced these energies as they invisibly flow in and around us.

Learning about the different energies and how they interrelate is a very useful way to understand our health, stress and disease. I will use energy to illustrate how to harness the power to change.

The Five Vital Energies of Change

The secret to creating successful change is summed up in the system I call the *EEEEEase to Success*™. Each "E" represents one kind of energy. This system and its percentages are based on my study of energy, my personal experience and the experiences of many of my patients.

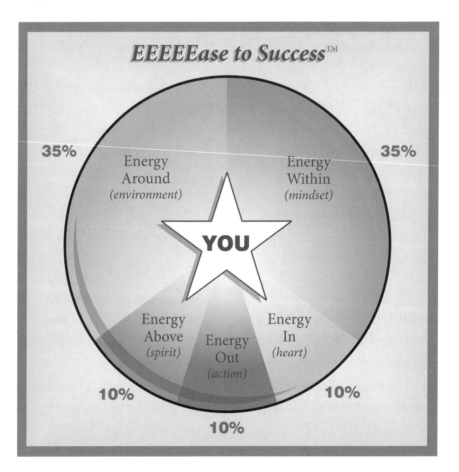

Most people think that the only energy we need to succeed in life is energy we generate outward—the action we take to move toward our goals. While this kind of energy is highly valuable, in my system, it accounts for only ten percent of the influence for change. There is another ninety percent of influence that is vital to create change more easily, effectively and permanently.

The remaining energies can be split into internal energies and external energies. Each category accounts for forty-five percent of the influence for change. The internal energies include the energy in you—also referred to as your heart—and the energy in your mind— also known as your mindset. The external energies include the energy around you, or your environment, and the energy above you, also known as spirit. Merging the internal and the external energies together allows you to step into the ultimate fifth energy—the energy out, which is the action you take.

Just like a battery, anything that drains energy is considered *bad* and anything that recharges energy is considered *good*. As discussed earlier, our cells are made up of energy. In that way, we are like a human battery. Negative energy, stress and anything else that drains our energy is considered unhealthy. On the contrary, positive energy and anything that builds up our battery is considered healthy.

Let's examine the five important energies in relation to *momentum*. Momentum is the accumulation of positive energy towards a goal. The higher the energies align in the same direction, the greater the momentum and outcome.

1. Energy In—Heart

Energy in refers to all the energy going into you. This includes that which nurtures your body, such as water, food, oxygen and nutrients, and that which nurtures your soul, such as celebration, accomplishments, gratitude and love. These relate to the heart in the way that what nurtures the body keeps the heart pumping and what nurtures the soul keeps the heart open.

Body nurturance. As you know, not all food and liquids that enter your body are the same. Do you know what happens if diesel fuel is poured into an unleaded fueled vehicle? The results are disastrous! In a similar manner, not all liquids are the same for our body. Water, is essential to all cells—to life itself. This is not the case with pop, coffee or juices. The more pure water you drink, the more healthy your body. The same is true for food. Organic, fresh, natural food is the healthiest for your optimal well-being. This is not true of processed, packaged or refined foods. Vitamins and minerals have been shown for decades to decrease disease such as heart disease, diabetes, osteoporosis and cancer. What you allow into your body matters. Choose wisely.

Soul nurturance. Acknowledging and sharing the good things in life goes a long way in supporting your energy and health. Making lists of your accomplishments and all you are grateful for nurtures your soul. Likewise, celebrating successes and expressing love adds to your success in life. Begin creating a list now, celebrating and expressing. (For information on how to create a gratitude journal, see Janet Wiszowaty's chapter, "Journaling at the Heart of Changing Your Life" on page 133.)

2. Energy Within—Mindset

One of the biggest factors that will determine your level of success is your mindset or *energy within*. For example, to lose weight, you know what is needed—eating healthier and exercising. However, what usually stops you from doing this is your mindset. Your mindset encompasses many factors, including your thoughts, feelings, attitudes, beliefs and habits.

Thoughts and feelings. These are the very basic energies within your mind. Do most of your thoughts support you to believe in yourself or are they excuses and explanations as to why you cannot create change? Do your feelings give you insight and information about what is going on internally or do they overwhelm you and keep you stuck?

Attitudes and beliefs. Attitudes and beliefs are simply thoughts and feelings with more energy, power and influence. The higher the energy attached to your thoughts and feelings, the higher the impact. This, in turn, creates your beliefs, which generates your attitude. Do your beliefs support you in positively and courageously moving forward or do they hold you back from going toward what you truly desire? (For more information on beliefs, see Beverly Lenz's chapter, "CPR for Your Soul" on page 11.) Do your attitudes call forth creative forces to assist you along the way or do they unconsciously push away all means of support?

Habits. Habits are automatic behaviors, tendencies, actions and reactions to the world around you. Often we assume habits are bad, such as smoking, cussing or lashing out in anger. However, there are also good habits like healthy eating, speaking kindly and practicing forgiveness. Do your habits nurture the highest well-being of others and yourself or do they sabotage you every step of the way, creating chaos around you?

> *"One person with a belief is equal to*
> *a force of ninety-nine who only have interests."*
> —John Stuart Mill, British philosopher, economist and civil servant

3. Energy Around—Environment

Your environment contributes to the *energy around* you. It is divided into the following five categories.

Home. Your home environment includes your physical space and the people within it. Your house, furniture, décor and the way everything is organized have an impact on your energy. If your home is cluttered, for instance, it contributes to a cluttered and disorganized mind. If there is beauty around you, it supports the beautiful qualities within you. The people in your home have a powerful impact on you as well—those who live there and those who enter the space. You are in control of your home and the energy you allow to affect you.

Work. Your job or work environment has a huge impact on your health and ability to manifest change. Do you have vending machines or poor air quality around you or do you work in a healthy and uplifting place? The people in and around your job affect your energy, happiness and productivity. You have control as to whether you allow the energy of your work to energize you or drain you.

Social network. Your hobbies, enjoyment and relaxation, as well as those you share your social time with, play an important part of your health. Do you spend your time with positive, encouraging, caring individuals or are you around people who complain, judge and deplete your energy? Do you choose to spend your free time in healthy environments that support your growth or do you socialize by drinking, eating poorly or watching too much television? The choice is always yours.

Professional network. Anything and anyone that gives you encouragement or skills enhances your ability to change. This category includes such things as inspirational books and CDs. It also includes trainers, dietitians, physicians, therapists, coaches—all those who have the extra skills and knowledge to support your highest growth. Are you incorporating tools that bring greater awareness to yourself and your contribution to life? Perhaps you can take classes or courses that invite you to grow more into who you most want to be.

Financial flow. You are likely aware that money, debt, savings and retirement plans can cause great stress and affect your mental, emotional and physical health. Financial stresses can also affect other parts of your life such as family, work, social life and the ability to seek outside support. If you have your finances in a healthy balance and flow, you can find support outside of you to reach your goals.

4. Energy Above—Spirit

Some people refer to our inner energy as our soul or spirit. Many believe that there is an all-encompassing energy source outside of us or perhaps deep within us—something bigger than ourselves. This source is referred by various names, such as God, Allah, Great Spirit, Supreme Being, Jehovah or Universal Life. Whether or not you believe in what I refer to as the *energy above,* practices such as prayer, yoga and meditation have shown to lessen stress and enhance mental, emotional and physical well-being.

5. Energy Out—Action Steps

The alignment and momentum of the internal and external energies coming together result in the ability to perform action steps, or *energy out,* with greater ease and success. Action steps are absolutely vital to becoming successful, yet they need the support of the other four energies. Think about how many times you have taken action steps toward your goal only to fail, stop or fall back into your previous patterns? It is because the other energies were not in place.

Creating the Change You Want

Assuming that all the energies are in place, let us examine the three important aspects of creating the change you want.

Accept responsibility. Examine the outcomes in all the areas of influence—the energy in, within, around, above and out.

- Are you happy with how your life is?

- Is there room for improvement?

- Do you accept responsibility for where you are now?

- Can you see that you are the only one who can make the changes necessary?

No more excuses, justifications or blaming. Accept full responsibility for your life!

Make a decision for change. Hoping for change, wanting change or wishing for change is not enough. These are all about living in the future. Decide and believe that you can change now and make the decision to do whatever it takes!

Be clear about your goals. The main reason for procrastination is not being clear on your goals, dreams or desires. Your brain works in the way a GPS, or global positioning system, works for a car and its driver. For example, if a driver tells the GPS to just drive for four hours, who knows where he or she will end up? However, if a driver programs the GPS to drive from Los Angeles to Las Vegas, he or she will end up in Las Vegas.

How much easier is it to plan and execute your goals if they are clear and specific?

Who allows what will and will not come into your body, heart or mind? *Who* chooses whether to ask the *energy above* for support? *Who* creates your environments and the people within your environments? *You!*

You are the star of your life. The star in the middle of the illustration on page 38 represents you! You have the power to make a difference in your life. Know the change you are aiming for! Then, create at least five action steps daily to move towards your desired life.

You hold many great treasures. You are worth it. All the power to you in your journey to your optimal life!

CAROL CONNICK, MD
Family Physician, Health Coach
and Stress Management Consultant

True happiness and health come from within!

(780) 481-7096
info@SOULutionsCoaching.com
www.SOULutionsCoaching.com

When Carol graduated from the University of Alberta, Edmonton, Canada, in 1992, and started working as a family physician, she quickly discovered the key cause of poor health—that was never taught in medical school—is stress—the energy of disease. Throughout her career in medicine, she realized that not all answers for health and happiness could be explained through traditional medical teaching, so she began exploring the characteristics of the mindset, beliefs and energy of the healthiest and happiest people.

In 2005, Carol created SOULutions Coaching, Inc., to advise corporate groups and individuals on stress and transformation as a framework for expanding greater health, happiness and productivity. She is a trusted expert who simplifies the complexities of medicine and explains how stress or negative energy anchors within the body to create disease.

With a medical degree and certifications in alternative health disciplines, Carol is uniquely qualified to address many aspects of stress. She delivers effective and easy techniques that enable patients and companies to transform stress, limiting attitudes and negative environments into empowering beliefs and productive habits, so they can be truly happy, healthy and whole.

Writing Intentions that Will Change Your Life

Unleash the Power Within

By Brett Dupree, CPC

The wonderful world that you live in is a plethora of spiritual information. Enlightening information that was once only available to the chosen few is now just a search term and a click away. Technological advances have created an environment that has advanced spiritual access to the point where you can obtain the same information as a king or a yogi who has trained for twenty years.

More information is on the Internet than anyone could ever assimilate. You can access millions of techniques, practices and philosophies right now. Within each of these techniques, practices and philosophies are hundreds of thousands of different inter-pretations. A simple search for "mindfulness meditation" brings more than 490,000 hits on Google®.

What does all this information mean? With each viewpoint on each philosophy, it is very easy to find two people who can read the same ancient text and give you a completely different interpretation. This problem is not just related to ancient texts. Even when reading books by current spiritual authors, such as Byron Katie, Deepak Chopra, Wayne Dyer and Eckhart Tolle, you will never be able to know exactly what they meant. It is left to your interpretation.

Enlightenment information is great and wonderful for the ancient yogis who have hours to meditate. You, however, have bills to pay. You struggle to figure out how to find five minutes of rest in your hectic life, let alone find time to discover who you are, meditate for sixty minutes, open your heart to unconditional love or live in the present moment. You cannot go on a two-week silent retreat. You have to take the trash out on Tuesday, pick up the kids from soccer practice and finish the report before the deadline.

How do you know what is right? With all this information, how do you know what is valid, real or legitimate? Even if it is correct, is it right for you? With so many voices, how can you determine the right one? How do you choose when they all seem so good?

My Right Choice

"The only real prison is fear,
and the only real freedom is freedom from fear."
—Aung San Suu Kyi, Burmese politician

I was once in the exact situation described in the quote. A few years ago, I was trapped in my own prison of fear, and I needed help. I was unable to have conversations with women, speak for myself, be honest with others and myself, have meaningful relationships and feel like I could be my true self. I just did not feel comfortable in my own skin, and I could not see a light at the end of the tunnel.

I felt hopeless and thought I would die alone with no meaningful contact in my life. A huge fear of abandonment was stopping me from being the person I knew I wanted to be. Then, at the age of 26, I decided I was ready to free myself from my prison of fear.

To break away from the prison, I utilized the Internet to purchase books, audio programs, workshops and online courses. As long as I kept searching, I found more and more information. I was making changes in my life. However, I was feeling overwhelmed by the amount of information and was frustrated that I was not making the significant change I sought. I needed some contact with real human beings who were successful at what they were doing. I needed to find the right answer for me.

One day, I decided to check out a local Intention Circle. An Intention Circle is a gathering where people meet to write down their intentions and support each other to become powerful at manifesting their wants and desires. After learning how to write intentions, I soon became a master at it. I was able to create intentions at a new level. They became joyous intentions that sang to my soul. My life began to align with these intentions and change for the better. I was able to become vulnerable with people and have meaningful contact. People began to ask me how I wrote my intentions and if I could help them with theirs. With the power of joyous intentions, I gained many friends, made meaningful connections, had conversations with strangers and used my fears for growth. Instead of being afraid of change, the future became exciting. All of the information that was available to me fell into place.

The Gift of Intentions

"Intention is a powerful force; the feeling of determination,
of really meaning it can move mountains!"
—Stephen Garrett, Canadian author, coach and consultant

The beauty of intentions is that they work on both your spiritual side and your rational side. Setting an intention will program your mind to point out to you what is meaningful for you. It is exactly like the new car effect. Do you ever notice that when you buy a new car, as if by magic, the car suddenly seems to be everywhere? Before you put your focus on the car, you never noticed that so many people owned that particular car. Now, you cannot go to the store without seeing three or four of them. This is the new car effect. Before you bought the new car, your brain did not care about the car's make, model or color. Once you owned the new car, the make, model and color became important enough for your brain to point it out.

Just like the new car effect, setting your intention will tell your brain what information is important to you. For example, when reading a personal growth book, the information that is relevant to your intentions will be brought to your attention. The words will be jumping off the page because they are what you need to take your spirituality to the next step in your evolution. What you learn from the book will mean more to you because the information aligns with your intention.

Instead of being overwhelmed by a plethora of information, you will now sift through it all and pick out the nuggets that fit your intention. Instead of being frustrated by Google returning almost 500,000 results, your brain will now point out what is interesting to you.

"A good intention clothes itself with power."
—Ralph Waldo Emerson, American poet and essayist

How to Write Joyous Intentions

Here are some important ingredients for writing down joyful intentions.

Know what you want. First, write down what you want. If you don't know what you want, you won't get it. Not writing it down is like getting into a car without a destination. If you drive long enough, you will eventually get somewhere. However, there is a good chance you will end up where you don't want to be. Know what you want. It is the most important step. For example, *Get out of debt.*

Be specific with the important details. Now that you have a destination, what do you want to do when you get there? When you read your intention, does it have specifics? Will you know when you are living your intention? For example, *I want to get out of debt and have enough money to enjoy myself.*

Get to the bottom line. What will this intention do for you? Getting to the bottom line allows you to understand the purpose of your intention. Write what you are getting out of the intention. You got in the car, and you know the details—now figure out why you are getting into the car in the first place. For example, *I want to get out of debt, so I can build my credit and feel relieved since I have enough money to have fun with.*

Write in present tense. It is time to act as if you are driving the car. Writing your intention in the present tense will program your brain and unleash the power of the Universe to align with your intention. Writing in the present tense is writing your intention as if your intention is already true. In this step, you will let the Universe and your mind know what you want and intend to receive, instead of asking for what you want. There is a big difference between driving the car and wanting to drive the car. For example, *I have great credit as I feel the relief of paying off my debt and having enough money to enjoy my life.*

Remove negatives from the intention. Remove roadblocks from the destination. Words have power. Each word in your intention is there to make you feel positive. Read your intention one word at a time and remove any word that does not make you feel good. In the example given, debt is a word that does not feel good when used. You can change it to, *I feel joy as I have great credit and am financially abundant.*

Add excitement. They say the journey is half the fun—now add the fun to your journey. This is the part where you make sure you get a giggle when you write your intention. Make sure your intention makes you feel great just by reading it. Add words that have great value to you. Have fun with it. For example, *I appreciate my wisdom as I am joyously living with great credit and am financially abundant.*

"Our intention creates our reality."
—Wayne Dyer, American self-help author and lecturer

How to Activate Your Joyous Intention

Your intentions are written. Now, it is time to activate them.

Create a ritual. Creating a ritual puts energy into your intention. A basic ritual is writing your intention down and hanging it on your wall, mirror or computer—somewhere where you will see it every day. Read it aloud at least once a day. Take the time to imagine what your life will be like when you are living out your full intention.

Increase your vibration. You can sing, meditate, dance to your favorite song or do any other action that increases your vibration. When you are vibrating on the same frequency as your intention, you will be given inspiration on how to bring the intention into your reality. You raise your vibration by feeling as good as you can. There is no need to try to feel joyful right away. Get to a joyful vibration in steps. As long as you raise your vibration, you are closer to getting what you want.

Release resistance. Let go of any resistance you have to your intention. The resistance is the negative emotions and thoughts that come up when you think of your intention. Have you ever noticed how you think of your best ideas when you are driving your car or right before you go to sleep? That is because on those two occasions, you are not paying attention to your thoughts, and you let go of resistance to your desires. When resistance does arise, meditate, go for a drive, watch television, pet your dog, go out in nature or engage in other activities that bring a feeling of relaxation.

Open to inspiration. Ask your inner wisdom for guidance and when you are on the same vibration as your inner wisdom, you will notice ideas pop into your head about your intention. This is called *inspiration.*

You will get amazing ideas. Write them down. Either keep a pen and paper handy or use your smartphone.

Create a task, practice or goal. Turn your inspiration into a task, a practice or a goal.

• A task is an action you can do right away or in one step, like reading an article.

• A practice is an action you do on a routine basis, like yoga.

• A goal is a series of tasks and practices for you to accomplish, like reading a book or creating a website.

Writing down your inspirations and turning them into tasks, practices or goals puts into action the Law of Attraction. The Law of Attraction states that what you attract into your life is based on the vibration you hold about it. Your vibration is based on how you think or feel about any given desire. The more emotion and positive thought you have toward a desire, the more the Universe will bring that desire to you.

What will likely happen is that you will find yourself feeling compelled to get your tasks and goals done, and they will be enjoyable to accomplish. The inspiration you gain comes from your own wisdom. You will do some tasks effortlessly. You will walk into a bookstore, a book will just call out to you, and you will buy it. Your life will be full of fun synchronicities, and your joy will increase.

Commit to writing one intention a week. With each new intention, you will take a step closer to living inspired. Living inspired will allow you to get into the flow of your life and just be. You will accomplish your goals in the most fun and easy way possible. Your intentions will allow you to surf the waves of personal empowering information. With each intention, your joy will increase. When your joy increases, you will increase the joy of the people around you. The joy of the people around you will expand, and then you will be a part of a joyous expansion that is sweeping this world. I invite you to truly live the life of your dreams!

BRETT DUPREE, CPC
Joyous Expansion™

*Increase your joy working
from the inside out!*

(253) 256-2144
brettdupree@joyousexpansion.com
www.joyousexpansion.com

Internationally certified life coach through inviteCHANGE,™ Brett envisions a powerful future in which people live in pure joy. He believes that there is a great, spiritual transformation just around the corner, and he coaches people on how to ride the powerful wave of awakening that is sweeping this world. Brett has dedicated his life to the study of personal empowerment. He believes that real, lasting change comes from changing from the inside out.

Working with people one-on-one, Brett helps spiritual seekers gain clarity on living their spiritual beliefs and personal values in their daily lives. He creates a sacred space that allows his clients to bask in the joy of creation. He helps them find peace and balance in their lives, so they can transform themselves into powerful beings. Using the power of intentions, the Law of Attraction and his deep, loving, powerful heart, he helps his clients gain miraculous results.

Brett is an inspirational speaker and has won awards delivering his powerful message of joy. You can find more inspirational words and videos on Brett's blog at www.joyousexpansion.com/blog.

Moving Forward after the Pain

Emotional Recovery and Relationships Following Sexual Assault

By Annalysse Gilbert

E verything in your life—good or bad—has a purpose and means something. This is a new twist to the well-known cliché, "Everything happens for a reason." With this understanding, you can embrace all events in your life and find deep meaning within them—even the most difficult and traumatic ones.

In 2003, my life as I knew it came to an emotional screeching halt when I attended a college football player's party and was incapacitated and raped by one of them. I remember most of it as if it happened just yesterday, and I suspect part of me always will. The scars from the cuts in my skin, though fading year by year, further solidify my nightmare. They also remind me that in my darkest moment—my most fragile, vulnerable and pivotal moment—came the chance for me to make a unique choice and foster character-defining strength. Although this chapter specifically focuses on a sexual trauma, this healing process can apply to any kind of trauma you have had in your life.

> *"Take the first step in faith. You don't have to see the whole staircase, just take the first step."*
> —Dr. Martin Luther King, Jr.,
> African-American civil rights leader

Three Critical Steps toward Healing and Picking Up the Pieces

With almost any traumatic event, there will be things you know you could have, or perhaps should have, done differently. The key is to not dwell on those things. Instead, take the necessary steps to heal from what happened.

I have resigned myself to the understanding that there are parts of that night I will never remember. I have since found how to heal and move on in a healthy way. I would like to share the critical steps of the healing process with you.

Step 1: Acknowledge to yourself what happened. Though most of us would like to forget what happened, repression is not a form of healing. When you think you are repressing something, your body will find another way for it to manifest—lymph swelling, body aches, sleeping problems, anxiety, depression, irrational fears, emotional, and often physical, reclusion and isolation. Acknowledge the truth and talk about it. Let yourself understand what happened and allow yourself to recall the assault. You may not like the topic—however, until you talk about it, it is not going anywhere.

Do not internalize it or be what I call an "emotional hoarder." Think about emotional hoarding like this: If you have rotten, molding food in your car stashed under the backseat, can you still smell it? Yes, and it worsens day by day. Does it putrefy and rot? Yes, exponentially, as time goes on. The same goes with repressing emotions. Just because you don't talk about them and cannot see them does not mean they are not overtaking your body, mind and emotions—consuming you like a malignant disease.

Step Two: Share with others what happened. This may be one of the hardest things to do, yet it is so important. Often, we hold unnecessary shame and just want the memory to go away. Understand that it will not go away—telling the right people about it is necessary if you want to move on.

If you are dealing with an assault, as I was, a crucial place to start is to report it to the police as soon as possible. I did not realize until working with law enforcement on a business level just how much of an asset the reporting of crimes is to the police and civilian communities. I, like many victims of crime, was scared, confused and embarrassed beyond description. I did not go to the police. In fact, I told no one for months. As a result, I found myself watching only crime shows, especially those with a sexual element. I did not sleep regularly and often watched *Law & Order: SUV®* all night and into the morning.

Despite knowing there is a certain level of embellishment surrounding the protocol and premise of such shows, I felt a kinship with every character in every story. I knew there would not have been a "Detective Olivia Benson" forcing her way through the double doors of the hospital with a compassionate smile and a calming voice, but it was my way of coping with not only the rape itself, but with my regret for not reporting it. Relating to these stories was all I had then. Knowing police officers the way I do now, I see I had nothing to fear back then. I should have involved the police immediately.

It is also important to share your story with others. Once I found the strength to speak about it, I immediately made the choice to share what happened any time it came up—in class lectures, debates, whenever and wherever I saw fit. I came to lend my voice to other women who had been brutalized and who were not ready to use their own voice.

I found solace, strength and courage in my own voice. You might start with someone close to you, or you might start with group therapy or a professional—someone better equipped to handle what you need to discuss who is less emotionally close to you. Any channel you can reach out to and talk it out with will expedite your emotional recovery.

Step Three: Forgive yourself and forgive the situation. This step can apply to any mistake you feel you have made although you will never be able to truly move on until you forgive the situation and, most of all, forgive yourself. Rape is never your fault. You did not ask for it. It was not what you were wearing, the way you were acting, how you were dancing or whatever else the case may have been. Being the victim of rape is one of the hardest things you will ever have to get through in your life—you must accept that it happened and forgive the situation.

I found that I had forgiven the situation within months of it happening. However, it took years before I could forgive myself. I was so angry with myself, thinking, *How could I have been so stupid to let this happen? How could I have been so weak to let some drug and some man take over me?* For years, I was angry and fraught with regret. I could not forgive myself for ignoring my initial instinct that something was not right at that party.

I cannot stress enough how therapeutic writing it all down can be for this step. Ask yourself questions and answer them. Write why you are angry or sad or whatever you are feeling and have a dialog with yourself. Do not hold anything in. Let it all flow through you and out of you—onto the paper and out of your head.

Take the time you need to heal. Timing is everything—and you have to do it on your own terms because you are worth every second. With life-changing events such as these, there is no mold, no absolute and no guidelines to follow. Everything after the fact must be done on your own terms. (For more information on forgiveness, see Yvonne Ohumukini Urness' chapter, "The Power of Forgiveness Using Ancient Hawaiian Wisdom" on page 143.)

Life after the Healing Begins

After you begin to find yourself in a stable emotional place, and the healing has started, it is only logical that you are going to want—and be ready to—foster relationships again, including an honest and attentive relationship with yourself. Here are some suggested steps to pave the way.

Find meaning in what happened. You may be thinking, *Are you serious? Find meaning in being raped?* Yes, I am serious. You cannot change that it happened. From your moment of greatest weakness, you will find that you have the strength and power to change this event into a character-defining moment in your life. You may not become a "caped crusader." However, you will find that you have a tremendous strength inside you. Now, you know that you are strong, powerful and can get through anything. You can now embrace the life you want and have the emotional foundation to choose what is right for you.

Build a relationship with yourself. You might find that your life prior to being raped is no longer a fit for who you have become after you were raped. For example, if you were an out-on-the-town person or a nightlife person, you might find that you are gravitating toward more demure activities or activities during different hours of the day. Perhaps you have changed with whom you associate.

It is okay to find new activities and grow other parts of yourself. However, if you find you are changing everything on an obsessive or avoidance level, you are likely falling into an unhealthy, introverted pattern. Self-exploration might need to take place under the guidance of a mental health professional. That is fine. This transition might be bigger than you can handle alone. Friends and family are a tremendous asset, yet often they cannot speak from an objective, psychologically healthy place. Part of knowing who is good for you is knowing who can best support you to move on in your life in a healthy, empowering way.

Step into an intimate relationship with caution and care. Intimate, sexual relationships are the next logical thing with which you might struggle. In my case, having emotionally lost contact with my brother, a once invaluable support, and physically losing my father to multiple deployments following *9/11*, I was already in a complete tailspin with the men in my life. Psychologically, the aftermath of my rape could have gone in two different extremes—my hating men completely or my finding validation solely from them. In my case, before and long after, I looked to men to save me, and worse, to complete me. This started a series of unhealthy, unsatisfying relationships, including two marriages by the age of 25. Ultimately, I found I needed to save myself. No one else can do this for you. Once you discover this, you will be in a place where you can have successful, reciprocated relationships.

Know who is good for you and who is not. We have instincts and often do not follow them! When you are ready to start meeting people and dating, make a list—literally. Write down all the things you want and, perhaps more importantly, things you do not want. Those do-not-wants are your red flags, so when you see one pop up, get out. Life is far too short to settle for less than you want or start something that, in time, will become stagnant or unhealthy. My list has 38 items on it—a tall order, and I know it will be more than worth the wait. Please be patient and know what is good for you.

Know your patterns. We all know a person who, no matter what, finds himself or herself with a cheater, a liar, a "bad boy" or a "bad girl" and cannot seem to understand why this always happens to them. It is simply a destructive dating pattern. This goes back to one of my favorite sayings, by Tony Robbins, "If you do what you've always done, you'll get what you've always gotten." Yes, you will—and that goes for dating, too! Recognize your unhealthy dating patterns and terminate them immediately when they start to happen.

Set boundaries. Boundaries are about respect. If you do not respect yourself, no one else will. While people can sometimes read signals, they cannot read your mind. Be vocal and do not assume someone will figure out what you want.

You must set boundaries—right from the start. Even before I was raped, and certainly after, I would tell anyone in the early phases of dating, "Do not lie to me or cheat. One lie, one slip up—I do not care the circumstance—we're done." This might sound harsh. However, trust is the most important boundary to me, and this has served me well. Know what your values are. You do not have to be demanding, rude or mean—simply state what you will and will not accept. It is as simple as that.

I cannot stress enough that when you are ready to explore an intimate relationship, you have to set boundaries. If people cannot accept your boundaries or respect your terms, they have no business in your life. It took me until I was into my early twenties. Now, I am enforcing boundaries and can spot patterns from a mile away.

Recently, I told a girlfriend, who had her own unhealthy patterns in relationships, "If you cover yourself with trash, no matter how hard you try, you are not going to make yourself smell like roses." The lesson? Even with the best of intentions, when you surround yourself with negative, toxic people, all you get are experiences and feelings that are negative, toxic and downright bad. It will not change unless you change it.

You have to remain true to yourself and know what you want. Do not be afraid to voice your needs and expectations—calmly, rationally and respectfully. Be introspective and demand respect for yourself. It is the foundation for everything you have and are about to delve into in your life.

Life Really Is Too Short

Whenever I used to stew over something, my mother would always tell me, "Turn the page, Anna." We laughed about it, yet her turn-the-page mentality has held true for many things in my life. I often take a couple steps further now and say, "Turning the page sometimes just isn't enough. Sometimes you have to close, or even burn, the whole darn book!" Life is too short to hold on to toxic events.

When my best friend, Sabrina, died in September 2009, her mother shared something with me that she read in one of Sabrina's journals. Sabrina wrote that she felt like she was living in a world where she was more dead than alive.

I am a writer, and I cannot find the words to explain the intensity with which that hit me. I remember the feeling of walking that line between emotional death and emotional life—and I, too, remember feeling more of the death and darkness than the light.

In a conversation years earlier, I remarked to a family member that I was astounded how, at such a young age, I was already looking at my failed relationships and the mistakes I had made. Hopelessly, I remarked, "If I could do it all over again!" I had so much baggage already! What he said changed my mindset immediately. He said, "Anna, it's only baggage if you keep carrying it around." Talk about a light bulb moment!

You truly do have the ability to turn the page and move forward. It really is your baggage only if you hold on to it and keep carrying it around. Let it go! Make the choice to drop it, or it will consume you. Please, do not be hard on yourself. Success in life is not always defined by the moments of great achievement, but, rather, by your character through great adversity. You truly have the power to change any event in your life.

ANNALYSSE GILBERT
Drive to Thrive

Success in life is not always defined by the moments of great achievement, but rather by your character through great adversity.

anna@drive-to-thrive.com
www.drive-to-thrive.com

I f laughter is the spice of life, you might consider getting yourself a bigger spice rack if you are going to share time with Anna, or Annalysse as her little Italian mother calls her. Love of laughter and infectious smiles are a constant theme in her everyday life. She believes in living each day to its fullest potential and taking whatever risk is necessary to achieve what the heart desires.

Anna is a graduate from the University of Nevada, Reno, with emphasis in journalism and psychology. There she took every chance she could to share her story and write strong pieces about it. Her feisty personality and open-book approach to sharing the tough times in her life have made her a great sounding board for victims of sexual assault, especially those who were too stigmatized or afraid to share their own stories.

Anna proposed and saw through her own advice column entitled "Ask Anna," which she wrote for the *Reno Gazette-Journal*™. She also contributed other articles aimed at self-improvement and building a happier you from the inside out.

Seven Universal Laws to Guide You to Personal Transformation

By Ed Dowling, MscD

I f are you are currently searching for more meaning in your life, realizing that something important is lacking, then you are probably aware that something needs to change. I have a secret for you—that something that needs to change is you. You can start the process of change by knowing and living in harmony with the seven Universal Laws. The laws will increase your wisdom and understanding of how the world works and will support you in your personal change or transformation.

One of the earliest teachers of personal change was Hermes Trismegistus, who lived in ancient Egypt about 4,000 years ago. An extremely wise man, he was the father of alchemy, astrology and psychology and was revered as a god by the Greeks and Romans. He gave us the seven laws to guide our quest for change. They are in operation every second of every day. They are the same everywhere. They do not favor some people or treat others unfairly. Living in harmony with them will help reduce your pain and unhappiness. As you allow yourself to be guided by these laws, you will develop a framework for personal change, and everything you learn will fit into it. You will be changing your life in an orderly, intelligent way. Your life will become easier, and you will become happier and more peaceful.

1. The Law of Vibration

This law informs us that everything is energy, which is in a continual state of vibration and motion. Energy exists in the form of sound, heat, light, electricity and magnetism. Matter, which is energy with a relatively slow rate of vibration, is found in the form of solids, liquids and gases. Everything has its own unique vibrational structure.

Scientists use three parameters to describe a vibration—its wavelength, amplitude and frequency. Imagine a vibration as being similar to a wave in the ocean. The distance between wave crests is its wavelength. The height of the wave above the normal sea level is its amplitude. The number of waves per unit of time is its frequency. Thus, there are millions and millions of possible different vibrations.

An understanding of this law will help you gain maximum benefits from working with all the laws. As you come to understand that everything is energy—your thoughts, words, emotions and actions—your vibrational frequency increases, and your change has begun.

Exercise. This exercise comes from a book by Penney Peirce called *Frequency: The Power of Personal Vibration*, published in 2009 by Atria Books. This exercise helps you get used to the idea that everything is a pulsating, throbbing, vibrating mass of energy.

• Start by sitting in a chair with your back straight, your feet firmly planted on the floor, and your hands open.

• Become aware of your breathing. Notice the rhythm of your breathing—in, then out, in, then out.

• Shift your attention to your heartbeat. Become aware of this faster rhythm. Your heart beats about once a second.

• When you are familiar with this faster rhythm, listen for a soft buzzing sound, probably in the area of your head. These are the sounds of the nerve impulses as they travel along your nerves and jump from one nerve cell to another.

Penney suggests that, as you practice this exercise, you will be able to detect the vibrations of your cells, and, eventually, the vibrations of the molecules and atoms making up your cells. It is all about fine-tuning your awareness to the vibrating energy of life.

2. The Law of Oneness

There is only one entity in the universe and that entity is called various names by different cultures, such as Universal Mind, Universal Consciousness and God. It fills up all space. It is everything that is, and there is nothing else. It always has been and always will be. Being a mind, it thinks. When it thinks of an object or an event, be it minutely small or huge, it is manifested. Universal Mind creates all things, and all things are a part of it.

Your mind is a part of Universal Mind. Consequently, you have the ability to manifest what you think about. Everything you create starts with one of your thoughts, which originates in your mind.

No one person is more important than any other. It is such a comfort to realize that every person is your brother or sister. Therefore, there is no reason to mistrust or be afraid of others. Everything you do for one other person, you do for everyone else. We are all one.

Exercise. This is an exercise to deliberately raise your personal vibration, enabling you to feel the connection and oneness in all, resulting in a happier, more peaceful you.

- For seven days, eliminate as much negativity as possible from your life. Replace any negative thoughts with positive ones. Avoid violent movies and television programs, particularly the news. Stay away from angry or pessimistic people. Look for and see only the goodness in yourself and others.

- Notice how you feel and what effect your state has on yourself and others. Pay particular attention to how you relate to the world around you.

- Record your experiences in a journal. As prominent transformational leader Robert MacPhee reminds us in his book *Manifesting for Non-Gurus,* published in 2010 by HeartSet Inc., "Journaling each day, capturing where we are in that moment, keeps us focused on where we are now while reminding us of where we are headed and how far we have come." (For more information on journaling, see Janet Wiszowaty's chapter, "Journaling at the Heart of Changing Your Life," on page 133).

3. The Law of Correspondence

The Law of Correspondence explains that the vibrations that make up Universal Mind form a continuum from extremely slow to exceedingly fast. The change you are seeking consists of increasing the frequency of your vibrations along this continuum. These vibrations are arranged into three main groups called planes. The slowest vibrations form the physical plane. Those immediately above it form the mental plane. The fastest vibrations make up the spiritual plane. These divisions are arbitrary because, as the Law of Oneness teaches us, everything is one. There is no distinct line of demarcation between planes. The physical plane merges gently into the mental plane, which gradually merges into the spiritual plane.

In the book *The Kybalion,* published in 1912 by The Yogi Publication Society, the authors, Three Initiates, remind us of the old teaching of

Hermes, which explains the Law of Correspondence as follows: "As Above, so Below; as Below, so Above." There is a correspondence and agreement between what happens on one plane and what happens on another plane. Whatever you think, say or do affects everything on all other planes. Therefore, you have the ability to change everything—the whole world even—with your thoughts, words and deeds.

The physical plane contains the vibrations that make up energy and matter. You can detect these vibrations with your senses of sight, sound, touch, taste and smell. The mental plane contains the vibrations associated with the minds of living things, not with their physical bodies. At one time, people believed that only humans were conscious. These days, most people are aware that animals are as well. Many realize consciousness is in plants, too—and sometimes talk to their house-plants and play music for them.

The spiritual plane contains the vibrations at the highest end of the continuum, which are those associated with the masters and adepts, the angels and archangels, and so on. The highest of these vibrations is pure light or pure love. Little can be said about this plane, as it can only be described and understood by people who have been there or who dwell there.

Implicit in the Law of Correspondence is the idea that the whole is contained in each part. Therefore, everything is related to everything else.

Exercise.

• For thirty days, make a deliberate effort to improve the health of your physical body, which is on the physical plane. Eat healthier foods and drink more water. Avoid or reduce your intake of junk foods, cigarettes, alcohol, sugar and coffee. Get some exercise, plenty of rest and avoid stress.

• Record how you feel on all three planes in your journal. Do you just feel better physically, or can you notice a corresponding improvement in your emotional and mental health, perhaps even in your spiritual well-being?

4. The Law of Polarity

Everything on all three planes has two poles and is dual in nature. There are two sides to every coin. Everything has its opposite. For example, on the physical plane, there is the concept of hot and cold. On the mental plane, there are the emotions of love and hate. On the spiritual plane, there is the idea of good and evil. There are many gradations between the two poles. Nothing is either one thing or the other. There is no one point where one polarity ends and the other begins. They are different degrees of the same thing.

Exercise. You can consciously choose to move along the continuum between any two poles on the mental plane. It is a very practical way of changing your life for the better. If you have hateful feelings towards someone, and those feelings are making you unhappy, you can decide to move along the continuum towards the opposite pole of feeling love towards that person.

• Think of someone you find difficult to love.

• Consciously look for something good about that person. This gesture will move you a little way along the continuum towards the love pole.

• As you think of a few good things about that person, more good things about them will emerge into your consciousness, moving you even further towards the love pole.

• As you continue this process, you will be able to move from hate, to dislike, to indifference, to like, to love—raising your own personal vibrations in the process and causing you to experience more happiness in your life.

• This exercise will also send positive, growing vibrations to the other person and uplift them as well. It is a win-win exercise that you can practice with any situation or person you find to be challenging.

5. The Law of Rhythm

Energy moves to its own unique rhythm on all three planes—first one way, then the other. These rhythms move along the continuum between any two extremes, as explained by the Law of Polarity. On the physical plane, the tide comes in and then goes out, the sun rises and then sets, the pendulum swings to the left and then to the right.

On the mental plane, your emotions also have their own rhythm. Consider a continuum with *happy* at one pole and *despair* at the other. You will probably experience times when you feel everything in your life is fabulous, causing you great happiness. Then, your mood swings in the opposite direction, and you may be plunged into despair. If you swing just a few degrees towards the *happy* pole then, on the return swing, you will move only a few degrees towards the *despair* pole. When this is the case, your life will generally have less stress, and you will be living a more even, balanced life.

Exercise. You can use the Law of Polarity to overcome any undesirable effects of the Law of Rhythm.

• If you have been very happy and notice yourself swinging back into depression, consciously remind yourself of the good times, thereby deliberately raising your vibrations towards the happy end of the continuum.

• Speed this process up by appreciating and being grateful for all the good people and circumstances in your life.

6. The Law of Gender

This law is concerned with generation or creation, which requires the creative force of the Universe to be active. As the Law of Polarity showed you, all things are dual or polarized, existing on a continuum. The creative force is likewise organized with the masculine force at one pole and the feminine at the other, sometimes called yin and yang.

Masculine and feminine energies are present in all people although the balance of the two forces may vary greatly in different individuals. Some people's creative energy may be concentrated towards the masculine pole, resulting in a take-charge, decisive type of person. Others may have this energy gathered towards the feminine pole and be more caring and nurturing. For creation to occur optimally, both energies must be present and balanced. The masculine energy naturally seeks out the feminine energy and fuses with it. Only then can creation occur.

Gender is expressed on all three planes. On the physical plane, there are positive and negative poles of electricity, and positive protons and negative electrons in atoms. On the mental plane, consciousness itself exists in male and female aspects. The conscious mind is the male part, directing itself towards the female subconscious mind. The conscious mind is required to have a vision and initiate action. The subconscious mind receives the vision and turns it into reality.

Exercise. In her book *Initiation,* published in 2000 by Aurora Press, Elisabeth Haich lists twelve pairs of opposite traits that an initiate was required to master and balance in order to enter into early Egyptian training for the priesthood. Shown on the following page are six of these pairs of traits, slightly modified, so that the traits in the first column are considered to be archetypal male characteristics, and those in the second column archetypal female characteristics.

According to Haich, it is necessary to be able to master each trait of each pair, to be able to express each trait at will and to have the wisdom to know when it is appropriate to express one trait while suppressing the other.

- Choose one pair of traits from the list above, for example, the *Talking-Keeping Silent* pair.

- Begin to work with this pair of traits in your conversations with others, taking note of your habitual patterns. For example, you can practice being talkative at times and silent at others. Observe when it is appropriate to speak up, such as when you witness an injustice, and when it is appropriate to keep silent, for example, when somebody is giving you feedback.

- Record your observations and feelings in your journal.

7. The Law of Cause and Effect

The Law of Cause and Effect states that every effect has its specific cause. Without the cause, there would not be the effect. Nothing is random. There is no such thing as chance. Chance is a term used by people when they cannot see the link between cause and effect.

One of the most valuable lessons you can learn from an understanding of the Law of Cause and Effect is that you are responsible for everything that happens in your life. America's success coach, Jack Canfield, writes in his book *The Success Principles,* published in 2005 by HarperCollins

Publishers, "The real truth—and the one lesson this whole book is based on—is that there is only one person responsible for the quality of the life you live. That person is you."

- Think of a time when you had a disagreement with someone, resulting in an unpleasant situation. If you blamed the other person for creating this situation, you likely made yourself a victim. You gave away your power. In order for the situation to improve, you required the other person to do the improving.

- Examine the events preceding the disagreement and determine what you did that contributed to it. Find your responsibility in the situation.

- Acknowledge your part in creating the situation and then be powerful by taking action to rectify it.

Now, you are aware of seven important Universal Laws that can guide you on your journey of personal transformation. If these laws are new to you, it might take several weeks, or even months, before the wisdom they contain sinks into your consciousness and becomes a part of you. You will likely need to read them again, perhaps repeatedly. As you begin to assimilate their wisdom, the frequency of your vibrations along the continuum of consciousness will increase. Your life will become easier and less stressful, and you will feel more love, happiness and peace. Congratulations! You are making powerful changes, and your personal transformation is now becoming a reality.

ED DOWLING, MscD

*Creating a firm foundation for
personal transformation*

(250) 377-1152
ed@edwarddowling.co
www.universallaws.co

A s a youth, Ed spent many hours exploring the natural surroundings of his home in England, which prepared him for his career as a high school biology teacher in Canada. Inspired by the first Earth Day™ in 1970, he pioneered one of the earliest Canadian high school courses in environmental education. He then joined the faculty of education at Simon Fraser University in Vancouver, British Columbia, training student teachers to introduce similar programs into their own schools.

Realizing that awareness of the outer environment begins with inner awareness, he studied gestalt therapy at Cold Mountain Institute in British Columbia, humanistic psychology at the Carl Rogers Institute at La Jolla, California, and Buddhism at the Library of Tibetan Works and Archives in Dharamsala, India.

Ed's current mentor is Jack Canfield, author and success coach. Ed received a doctor of metaphysical science degree from the University of Metaphysics in Sedona, Arizona. He offers easy-to-understand metaphysical counseling to individuals and small groups, concentrating on creating a firm foundation for personal transformation by living in harmony with the natural laws of the universe.

Changing Your Wealth Beliefs and Stepping into Success

By Byron Ingraham

D id you ever hear the expression, "Money doesn't grow on trees?" Maybe you were even told that "Money is evil." If your childhood was similar to mine, you probably heard expressions such as these that, ultimately, had a profound effect on your life and how you now view money. Although the intention of sharing these expressions may have been to protect us from harm—from getting hurt, disappointed or disillusioned—what they did was create a barrier in our minds for getting what we truly want in life.

Most of us are not taught to take risks and go for what we want. How many times have you found yourself not doing something for fear of failing or hurting yourself? Naturally, we want to avoid pain and discomfort, yet it is our beliefs about pain and discomfort that ultimately affect the success or failure we experience on a daily basis.

In this chapter, you will focus on the beliefs that hold you back from creating the lifestyle of your choosing and affect the wealth that you do or do not have. You will get a clear picture of what it is that you truly want and lay the foundation for getting there.

Eliminating Limiting Beliefs about Wealth

Let us start by taking a look at where the foundation of our belief systems began. As children, we modeled the people around us—mainly our parents and other adults of influence. We learned from them how they lived their lives and what they said to us and others about money and wealth. From this impression, our own beliefs were created.

Answer these questions to help you gain some insights into the foundation of your beliefs on wealth.

• Who were the five most influential adults in your life when you were growing up?

• Make a list of what you learned from them about money or wealth. What did you witness or hear?

• What about your life now resembles these people from your past?

This exercise will show you the beliefs that were created about wealth from your upbringing. The good news is that you now have the opportunity to change the beliefs that do not empower you to succeed. One simple, yet important way, to do that is to notice when you have a limiting thought about money and change that thought immediately into something positive and supportive. Eventually, this new thought will become stronger than the old thought, and your life will change for the better. For example, you may find yourself drawn to a luxurious item, such as a car or a nice house. You may automatically think, "I could never afford that." You can change this into the new belief, "I deserve that and more, and I have the ability to manifest good things in my life."

Setting Goals

We are living in a fast changing world, and the belief systems that people held for the previous fifty years do not hold now. For example, in the past, people expected to have a pension from whatever job they worked for thirty years. Now, it is up to the individual to provide for his or her retirement. Times are changing, and we have to change with them.

To truly create the wealth you want to attract in your life, you will have to take massive action. Things will only get better if you decide that they will and if you are ready to do what it takes to make them happen. One of the first things you must do is to set big, audacious goals. When setting goals, *focus on the destination—not on how you are going to get there.* Many times when we start working towards a goal, we do not always have the tools or the knowledge necessary at the beginning. This comes with time. Along the journey, we gain the knowledge and the experience needed to achieve our goals. Here is a two-step process to help you set and achieve your goals.

• Create a list of 101 goals that you truly want to achieve or have in your life.

• Create a list of 51 people that are in your life who are a positive influence and are goal oriented.

The purpose behind creating a list of 101 goals is to have something to work toward. When you have goals that you want to achieve in life, you tend to work harder and smarter to make them happen. You have probably heard that if you write down your goals, they are more likely to be achieved. Often, when you set and write goals, you acquire the resources needed to make the goal possible, or you learn the skills needed. By writing them down, you will do something that the majority of the population does not do.

Creating a list of 51 people in your life who are a positive influence will help you achieve your goals. The aim is to reach out to as many of these people as possible, find out what their main goals in life are and help connect them with the people and the resources they need to make their goals possible. By taking an active interest in other people's lives, it is more likely that others will take an interest in yours and help you. It is a natural giving and receiving process. Imagine you are trying to achieve all your goals on your own. Imagine others are trying to achieve all their goals on their own. It does not create a very promising picture. The truth is—we need each other. Supporting each other is a very powerful force of change that can completely alter your life.

The Importance of Mentors

Creating the wealth you desire in life requires that you grow to become more than who you are today. One of the best ways to achieve this is to seek out mentors who are already achieving what you want to accomplish and begin doing the things they have done to get to where they are in life. Finding the right mentor will reduce the amount of time to reach your goals. This is done through modeling their behaviors, thoughts and actions.

People who are successful will typically think a certain way that is different from how most people think. When something unexpected happens in your life, do you see it as a problem or an opportunity? Successful people will typically see unexpected situations as opportunities.

A mentor does not always have to be someone who is directly in our lives. One of the greatest sources of mentors can be found in a library. Libraries have large volumes of biographies on influential people throughout history, such as former presidents, business leaders, inventors and so on. You can learn an amazing amount from reading about influential people.

Here is an exercise to help you identify the mentors in your life.

• List five to ten of the most successful and influential people currently in your life.

- What do these people do and why is it important to you?

- What types of activities do they do in their lives?

- How are you currently different from them?

- What can you learn from them or model after them?

- Why do you want to change or enhance who you are in order to become the person you are fully capable of becoming? What are your motivating reasons?

This last question is an incredibly important one. Knowing the *why* behind what you do will fuel you to continue to move toward your desired goals and reach your true potential. No one can tell you or force you to become something or someone that you do not want to be voluntarily. You must make this decision on your own.

Changing Your Environment

Along with identifying your chosen mentors, you must also look at the environment you are currently in to understand if it is supporting your new endeavor or holding you back. Just as you identified five to ten mentors to model in life, you must identify the five to ten people you currently spend the most time with outside of your family. Your success and income will be directly tied to the people you spend the most time around. If you want to increase the level of success you are having, start spending time with those who are more successful than you are. You will notice differences in the activities they do on a daily basis as well as their belief systems and the connections they have.

Often, people who do not begin to change who they spend time with are held back by those who are currently in their lives. It is not necessarily because these people do not want to see you succeed. It may simply be because they do not know how to support you in a different way, or perhaps they fear losing you.

One of the best ways you can have the support you need as you embark on your journey to create wealth is to start a Mastermind® group. A Mastermind is a group of like-minded individuals focused on helping each other achieve their goals in business and in life. Your Mastermind group should be made up of people who are all on a similar journey and who want to offer and receive support for their goals. This group can become your new peer group—a group of like-minded people with whom you spend more and more time as you move towards your goals. One of the greatest things that will happen is that a greater number of opportunities will begin to present themselves to you because of your newfound connections. Always remember that like attracts like.

Fueling the Change through Knowledge

Fueling your mind with the right kind of knowledge is critical for creating growth that leads to changing your belief systems about wealth. One of the simplest ways to fuel your mind is to spend time each and every day on personal growth. Far too often, people will use the excuse of not having enough time during the day to do uplifting activities such as reading. According to Nielsen, a global marketing and advertising research company, in 2009 the average American watched approximately five hours of television per day. That works out to be approximately 76 full days a year spent in front of the television. Take into consideration that the average school day is 6.7 hours a day. This means that the average person is spending almost as much time watching television as a student spends learning in school!

I invite you to become a student of wealth. Challenge yourself to study about wealth at least thirty minutes a day. Reduce or eliminate activities that do not help you reach your goal. For example, you may choose to reduce the amount of time watching television, checking Facebook® or watching YouTube® videos. Invest in your education by buying educational books, audios and videos. Listen to inspiring recordings on the CD player in your car or on your mp3 player when you are walking.

Read supportive books while you are waiting at the doctor's office or before bed each night. Attend workshops or courses that strengthen your mind and encourage you to step into your greatness and brilliance!

Taking Big Leaps

Everything that you have learned up to this point is designed to help you lay the foundation for creating wealth. The critical piece that you must integrate is the belief that you can do something you have not done before. Accomplishing something in your life you thought was not possible is a critical step. When you start believing in the possibilities in life, instead of the limitations, you will experience a total shift in how you view the world around you. I have listed some of the things that many people identify as something they would never do.

• Walk on fire

• Bungee jump

• Sky dive

• Speak in public

• Break wooden boards with their bare hands

The above list is just an example of what many people think are impossible to do or things they would rather avoid in life because they do not believe in themselves. It is time to take action and change your beliefs by conquering something that you fear . The more you believe in the rich array of possibilities in life, the more opportunities will come your way.

Creating Wealth

In the book *The Millionaire Next Door,* by Thomas J. Stanley and William D. Danko, published by Pocket Star Books in 1998, the authors state that the majority of millionaires in Western society are self-employed. Have you ever wondered why some people work all their lives for someone only to be paid a fraction of what they are worth? Ask yourself two simple questions:

• How much am I making in my career right now?

• What do I believe I am worth?

Ultimately, you will not make more in life than what you believe you are truly worth. If you walk around saying, "I'm just not good enough," then that is what you will be—not good enough. However, you can decide right now that you are truly worthy. You must make it your mission to turn what you feel you are worth into reality. You are the only one who can make this happen.

The most important thing you can do is to simply get started on your journey to create wealth. You do not need to know exactly how you are going to do it, you just need to know with certainty that it is what you want and that you can do it. A great example of this kind of thinking happened in the 1960s with the United States space program. In a speech given by President John F. Kennedy, on May 25, 1961, he stated that an American was going to the moon. This was something that had never been done before. There was just a vision. New knowledge was needed, and skills had to be learned to make the vision possible. That vision was achieved on July 20, 1969.

What we can all learn from this historic event is that if we dedicate ourselves to achieving our goals in life and acquire the resources needed to make it happen, anything is possible.

Fear of Failure

One of the things that can hold us back from achieving our goals, and even paralyze us, is the fear of failure. However, if you look at the most successful people throughout history, you will find that they failed at something at some point in their lives—perhaps they had many failures. However, those failures did not stop them.

Let us look at the sport of baseball. If a baseball player has a batting average of .350, they are considered to be an amazing player. What we tend to forget is this—they miss or fail to hit the ball 65 percent of the time when they are at bat! What we can learn from this is to not be afraid to take risks in life and go for what is most important to us. There will be plenty of times that we miss or seem to fail, yet there will also be times when we hit a home run in our endeavors and create great wealth! My strongest advice to you is to trust the process and trust yourself.

You are at the beginning of an amazing journey of transforming your beliefs about success and creating wealth in your life. To achieve the wealth you are seeking, it is up to you to make it happen. Start today!

BYRON INGRAHAM
Speaker, Coach, Author

(972) 836-9503
byron@byroningraham.com
www.byroningraham.com

Helping people around him reach their full potential has been a hallmark of Byron's life. He served in the United States Air Force for ten years, developing highly profitable business plans and strategies for hotels, restaurants, fitness centers and retail operations located on air force installations around the globe. In 2007, Byron moved to Plano, Texas, knowing only one person. He has built a network of thousands through collaborative networking and helping professionals achieve the business results they seek to achieve.

Byron is a solid believer that our thoughts shape the world around us and, ultimately, define the level of success we experience in life. This philosophy has consistently led him to guide teams to change their belief systems on what is possible and achieve greater results in the workplace. He dedicates time each day to his own personal development to reach new levels of achievement.

Currently, Byron works with business owners to develop strategies that increase their levels of success and profitability. His energy and engaging presence make his presentations on business development fun, entertaining, exciting and highly informative. He is an avid cyclist, social media aficionado and dynamic business leader.

The Power of Essential Oils to Change Your Life

By Lynn Kwitt, RMT, CCA, CWC

Many people have traumatic experiences in their life that can either lead them to deep despair or to a level of healing that is actually connected to their life purpose. I had such an experience in my life. With great effort and determination, I chose an alternative road that led to my own healing and gave me the gift of helping others to heal as well.

In this chapter, I will share some powerful stories that brought about change with essential oils. I will also describe where these oils come from and how you can use them in your own life for healing yourself, or, if you are a practitioner, for healing others.

My Story

At eight months of age, I became paralyzed on my right side. It made life awkward for me growing up. I was quiet and introverted. While the other kids were running around chasing each other, I physically could not participate as they could. Part of my body could move—and the other half could not. The doctors thought it might be cerebral palsy and experimented on me with drugs that produced unwanted side effects.

At nineteen, a CAT scan revealed that I had, in fact, suffered a stroke. *I did not have cerebral palsy.* I soon began searching for alternatives to the pharmaceuticals that were exacerbating the problem. It wasn't until I discovered reiki that my body began to find balance, and I began to gain movement on the right side of my body. The real turning point, however, came when I started using Young Living Essential Oils™, the nation's largest distiller of essential oils. The peppermint oil I started to use began to regenerate my nerve endings, and the oils, in general, helped more oxygen reach my brain. I now have about seventy-five percent of the feeling back on my right side. The more I use the oils, the more I continue to heal.

I immediately started to use them as an adjunct to my reflexology and reiki practice with good results. Now, I promote essential oils and other healing modalities. As long as oils enter your system topically, internally or through inhalation or diffusion, which is described later in this chapter, they can correct most ailments by balancing the system naturally. You will learn the various ways essential oils may help you, from minor cuts to cleansing your environment.

> *"All cure starts from within, out, from the head down,*
> *and in reverse order as the symptoms have appeared."*
> —Constantine Hering, American homoeopathist

Essential Oils as a Natural Solution

Nature provides all the means by which we can heal the physical body, as well as the soul. My approach to health is to naturally support all of the organs and systems of the body that are directly and indirectly connected to each other and to the soul. Essential oils are the perfect bridge to heal the body on all levels—physical, psychological, emotional and spiritual.

Distilled from flowers, stems, leaves, roots and even resin, unadulterated essential oils are the only substance that can raise the body's electrical frequency above disease level. Therapeutic-grade essential oils are not to be confused with most of the essential oils on the market in the United States today. This higher grade means the plant must be grown organically or in the wild under ideal conditions. After the plant material is gathered, it must be distilled at the right temperature for the exact amount of time, so the proper chemistry is not burned off.

I cannot stress enough the delicate vital chemistry that is needed for essential oils to contain the life force essential for healing. Even one drop of alcohol, camphor or other additive will render the healing properties in the essential oil inactive. In addition, if any of the compounds are burned off during the distillation process, its chemical components will be compromised. Therefore, it is important to make sure you use therapeutic-grade essential oils only. When the label says "one-hundred-percent pure essential oil," it means only one drop of pure oil is required in the bottle. The rest can be additives. The oils I will be referring to in this chapter are based on the French model of aromatherapy, specifically Young Living Essential Oils.

Essential oils can be used alone or as an adjunct to other healing methods. They increase the effects of healing synergistically to the user's benefit. For example, using lavender in an acupressure session on any one of twenty-six acu-points can increase its effectiveness. If you are a healer, just getting oils on your own hands creates additional benefits.

"Anything essential is absolutely necessary—a fundamental requisite to healthier living. Essential oils are nature by the drop, to enjoy and enhance life."
—Colleen K. Dodt, American herbalist

Sally's Story

Sally came to see me for two reasons. First, she was interested in creating more abundance in her life. Her business wasn't really making a profit, and her roommate was not paying rent. Second, she had experienced a violent and traumatic rape forty years prior where she was locked in a closet for almost eight hours. Though she had worked through much of the trauma, she still could not bring herself to open closet doors. Her goals were to make more money, clean out a bedroom closet and make room for a new housemate.

I used my education as an aromatherapist and my intuition to come up with some solutions. First, I recommended diffusing Valor® in her living room to give the current housemate strength and courage to either leave or pay rent. I recommended Sally use Valor on her feet before bed when she felt insecure. Next, I had her use Abundance™ oil on her heart center points while saying the affirmation, "I ask and I accept." Next, we used Release™ essential oil under her Adam's apple with the affirmation, "All things happen at the perfect time." Grounding™ essential oil was used at the top of the tailbone with the affirmation, "I connect with my inner knowing." She also used ginger and Aromasiez™ at recommended times during the day for a period of weeks.

Sally started using the oils immediately and began to feel a shift in energy within one week. She said her roommate paid her all the money he owed to her plus extra for utilities. Her friend bought $200 worth of training materials from her online site, and her father-in-law gave her $1,000 toward care for her disabled son. She gained a total of $2,000 in just the first week! Within a month, she had emptied the closet and another roommate had moved in. This shows the true potency of essentials oils for our well-being on all levels.

Some Benefits of Using Therapeutic-Grade Essential Oils

• Promote overall health, vitality and longevity. Essential oils oxygenate the cells of the body and aid in maintaining normal cellular regeneration. They support the body's natural defenses by building the immune system, and they have antiseptic properties.

• Create an overall sense of well-being. Essential oils improve mental clarity and elevate your mood. They help manage stress and frustration and help you relax.

• Boost stamina and energy. Essential oils create more energy by rebuilding and balancing the systems of the body.

• Beautify and clarify the skin. Essential oils reduce the appearance of aging. The healing properties of essential oils normalize the cells including those of the skin, which is the body's largest organ.

How to Use Essential Oils

As mentioned at the beginning of the chapter, there are four ways in which you can use the oils: topical, inhalation, diffusing and internal.

Topical. When applying directly on the skin, it is best to first test the inside of your elbow to see if there is any skin sensitivity. If so, you can dilute the essential oil with a vegetable oil, such as olive or jojoba oil. Topical methods include massage and various other healing modalities like acupressure. Use in a cold or warm pack or a compress. Add to the bath or shower by mixing with an unscented bath or shower gel or by adding the oil to Epsom salts. Layer oils by applying one over another for added benefits. Below are some suggestions.

• **Grapefruit or juniper oil.** Use one or two drops of grapefruit or juniper oil in Epsom salts in a morning bath to wake you up and feel energized throughout the day.

• **Panaway® or Aromasiez oil.** Use one of these blends to loosen tired, sore muscles by massaging the skin.

• **Lemon oil.** Lemon oil is a natural cleanser and removes toxins, whether from your lymph system, skin, internal organs or blood stream. Apply topically anywhere on the body. The feet are the most absorbent part of the body. Essential oils have an innate intelligence. They go where they need to go, and the rest dissipates.

Inhalation. Smell the oil directly by placing two or three drops in your hands and rub together. Cup hands over your nose and mouth and inhale deeply. Here are some suggestions.

• **Neroli, orange blossom.** When inhaled, this oil changes your brain waves to theta brain waves, relaxing you immediately. It contains natural antidepressant qualities and is mood balancing. It is useful for emotional shock, aids in sleep and helps lift the spirits.

• **Trauma Life™.** Use this for physical or emotional trauma. It acts like smelling salts, reviving you instantly. When smelled or applied topically at the base of the head, where the neck meets the head, it may re-establish harmony by emotionally and physically correcting the root cause. It can normalize the cells, balancing the body on all levels to 100 percent.

• **Peppermint.** One drop of this Young Living oil is equal to 28 cups of tea. Try smelling it from the bottle first thing in the morning to keep you going all day.

Diffusing. You can use a cold air nebulizing diffuser, which is designed to atomize a fine mist in the air. You can also use the oils in a humidifier or vaporizer. Add essential oil to cotton balls and put in vents to clean the air. Add to cedar chips and make your own potpourri. Place a bowl of water on a wood stove and add a few drops of essential oil. Never burn therapeutic-grade oil using a candle or any form of heat. It will take away the healing properties of the oil.

- **Cedarwood oil.** Use cedarwood oil on cedar chips to improve concentration, take away odors, especially pet odors, and cleanse the air.

- **Frankincense.** Use this oil in a nebulizing diffuser for meditation and to obtain higher states of consciousness. It can be used in place of incense and has a high level of potency.

- **Purification® oil.** This is a special blend formulated to neutralize odors, eliminate bacteria and cleanse the air. Put the oil on cotton balls in vents when traveling. It can eliminate the smell of cigarette smoke.

Internal. Taking an essential oil sublingually—under the tongue or on the inside of the cheek—has the greatest absorption rate—up to ninety-five percent. *Again, this is specifically with Young Living therapeutic-grade oils only.* Put a drop or two in soymilk, on bread or mix in other foods. Internal absorption is best done only after you have used therapeutic-grade oils in other applications with comfort over time. Please check the label to make sure the oil is safe for taking internally. For extended use, consult a physician.

- Put one drop of oregano and one drop or more of vegetable oil in an empty vegetable capsule, found at health food stores, and take internally several times a day to help prevent bacterial infection from water when traveling out of the country. Caution: Always dilute oregano and use sparingly until you feel what amount is right for you.

- Add one drop of nutmeg oil to your smoothie to balance the adrenal glands. Add grapefruit oil to one teaspoon of honey to cleanse the kidneys and lymph and vascular systems.

" . . . And the fruit thereof shall be used for meat,
and the leaf thereof for medicine."
—Ezekiel 48:12, *American Standard Bible*

Medicinal Use

Many people use essential oils for medicinal purposes. Please note that these statements have not been evaluated by the Food and Drug Administration, and the products are not intended to diagnose, treat, cure or prevent any disease.

- **Cold and flu prevention.** Oils like thyme, oregano and Thieves® oil may help build the immune system.

- **Pain management.** Clove, wintergreen, peppermint and panaway blend produce a cooling effect and penetrate deeply into the system to help with inflammation, pain and arthritic conditions.

- **Basic first aid.** Lavender has been used successfully for centuries on cuts, bruises, burns and scrapes. It speeds healing and may reduce pain. Panaway is used for pain and swelling. It helps prevent infection and may reduce bleeding.

Common Household Use

Essential oils are used in the making of several household items, such as paint, paper, rubber, plastics, textiles, insecticide preparations and adhesives. Here are some ways you can use them at home.

- **Lemon oil.** Use lemon oil to take off adhesives from labels that have left a mark on bottles.

- **Thieves oil.** Use Thieves oil in pure water or with vinegar and water in a spray bottle to clean surface areas, neutralize odors and disinfect naturally.

- **Purification oil.** Put about sixteen drops in a can of paint to neutralize the fumes.

Cooking Use

Essential oils are excellent for cooking. Please remember that if you use oils for cooking, choose only therapeutic-grade oils that specify internal use.

- **Basil, thyme and rosemary.** Use these sparingly for cooking. Remember, one drop is enough to flavor whatever you are making. You can use these oils to flavor soups at the end of preparation.

- **Orange, cinnamon and lemon oil.** Use these to flavor baked goods. Add lemon oil to water when out at a restaurant to neutralize the chlorine content or add one drop to tea with honey instead of a lemon slice.

- **Peppermint oil.** Add one drop to warm water or to any tea for a pick-me-up or to settle the stomach.

Recommendations

When using essential oils for acute or immediate conditions, try using one or two drops every hour. As symptoms lessen, use less often. Some oils, like cinnamon and oregano, are hot oils. Pair with a vegetable oil in at least a 50/50 dilution, so they will not burn the skin. Some oils are photosensitive, like bergamot, angelica and citrus oils, so do not go out in direct sunlight after using topically.

Store oils in dark glass bottles in a cool location away from light and children. Make sure the lids are tightly closed to prevent evaporation, as these oils are liquid. If you get an essential oil in your eyes, use a vegetable oil to take out the sting. Water will inflame the effects.

Now that you know the value of using essential oils, I invite you to experience them for yourself. Add them to your medicine cabinet, your kitchen, your bedroom and your cleaning supplies. Don't leave home without them!

LYNN KWITT, RMT, CCA, CWC

The Joy of Essential Oils

(707) 570-0751

lynn@thejoyofessentialoils.com

www.thejoyofessentialoils.com

C lients call Lynn the embodiment of a twenty-first century medicine woman. In her practice and through teaching the art and science of holistic health, Lynn combines her vast knowledge of therapeutic-grade essential oils with her intuitive hands-on techniques.

During twenty years of professional social work, Lynn's career naturally evolved into healing. Her practice today draws on the scientific and the intuitive. She considers each case individually, assesses specific needs and offers solutions for each person. Solutions could include activities from writing and drawing to affirmations or movement, along with appropriate bodywork, including reflexology, raindrop technique massage or reiki. She also offers intuitive wellness consultations by phone to help determine the most effective therapeutic-grade essential oil for individual cases. Lynn has been a Young Living Essential Oil™ distributor since 2000.

Lynn lectures and offers interactive classes and workshops focusing on raising natural vibrations, frequencies and energy. Her specialty is helping the externally-driven client regain his or her heart center, self-understanding and inner balance. She enjoys writing, reading, teaching and cooking with essential oils. Currently, she resides in Sonoma County, California, where wine is considered a food group.

What You Eat Matters

Three Easy Steps to Extraordinary Health

By Debra Liddell, CDC, CFH, CNH

I meet people every day who have physical pain and are hurting in different ways. They do not feel good, they have little energy, and they tire easily. Their joints hurt. They are overweight and are often struggling with some disease. They feel they have lost control over their lives and are at the mercy of whatever happens to them. They wonder if this is as good as it gets. I personally have been there. I suspect you, too, may be able to relate to some or all of this, as well.

As a nutritional family herbalist and coach, I know that it does not have to be this way. You can take control of your life. You can take control of your family's life and live a life of extraordinary health.

Extraordinary health is not about treating diseases. It is about being disease free. You can free yourself from being overweight, in pain, tired and plagued with disease. You have everything you need within you to have an extraordinary, healthy life.

When you take control and responsibility, amazing things happen. As your health improves, you will find yourself doing things you thought you could never do. You will find self-reliance and confidence as you realize you are making choices and changes to transform your life. All you need are a few tools and some guidance. Let me start you on your way with three beginning steps and some amazing ways to use food.

"Now I see the secret of the making of the best persons.
It is to grow in the open air and to eat and sleep with the earth."
—Walt Whitman, American poet

Cleanse, Nourish, Heal

Let us first look at how you got to where you are. As a baby, you were born healthy and clean. Then, you were exposed to environmental toxins as you grew and developed. Your body took on years of abuse with processed foods, refined sugars, fast food and chemicals. You ate nutritionally depleted food. When you eat food that is deficient, you become deficient in nutrients. It is the accumulation of toxins in your body and a lack of nutrients that are responsible for the increasing problems with your health.

Changing old habits and learning new ways can be a challenge. With my three steps of cleansing, nourishing and healing, you will discover how you can have a long, healthy and active life. To cleanse is to make the body thoroughly clean by removing toxins. To nourish is to give the body the nutrients it needs to live, grow and be healthy. To heal is the process of becoming healthy and disease free. Now, let us examine them more closely.

Cleanse. Cleansing the body is the first step towards having a healthy body. It is important to rid the body of the toxins that have accumulated over time. A cleanse needs to be natural so as not to add to the toxins already in your body. Several different combinations and methods will give good results. In ancient times, people cleansed by fasting. In Native American cultures, a sweat lodge was used. These methods are still used today in cleansing.

Imagine looking at a car with a dirty engine. There is grease and grime built up everywhere. The performance of the car has been compromised. The engine may rattle, and its efficiency will be low since it will use more fuel and probably see the junkyard before its time. Now, imagine the same car if you have taken the time to keep the engine clean, replaced dirty oil and used a high-grade fuel. In this case, you have a car where fuel consumption is lower, and performance is higher. This car will last longer and have fewer breakdowns than the dirtier car.

Think of your body as this car. Accumulated toxins over the years will keep your body from being efficient. It will break down faster than it should. Changing your diet, on the other hand, will start a natural cleansing effect. When your body is clean, you will receive the full benefit of nutrient-dense foods and herbs.

The body has four basic channels to cleanse itself: the skin, the respiratory system, the bowel and the urinary system. A cleanse that gets down to the cellular level is what is needed to truly rid the body of the toxins throughout it. This process takes time and can be painful because toxins are stored in the weakest part of your body. An herbal nutritionist can assist you with the herbs and herbal formulas that will cleanse your body on a cellular level and make your experience gentler and more beneficial.

> *"Your food shall be your medicine*
> *and your medicine shall be your food."*
> —Hippocrates, Ancient Greek physician

Nourish. What you will or will not eat is one of the free choices that you have to make. After cleansing, it is important for you to nourish your body by giving it the nutrients it needs. Everything you put into your body needs to build it up, not break it down. Nutrition from real food and herbs do this.

When I was young, I broke seventeen bones. Thankfully, I did not break them all at once! My mother said that I was always a tomboy or daredevil. She was right—although the things I did should not have broken my bones so easily.

Looking back, I realize my bones were weak, even though I was a big milk drinker. I ate the average American diet, which included refined sugars, white bread, processed foods, dairy and meat—food that was nutritionally depleted. It was not real food. Therefore, my bones were weakened. Real food is not processed—it is in its natural form. It is dense with the nutrients your body needs.

There are three different factors about food to consider as you plan what you put into your body.

- **Raw is better than cooked.** Cooking food kills the enzymes and nutrients that your body needs. By the time your food gets to your plate, it is nutritionally depleted. The molecular structure has changed and may appear as a toxin to your immune system, causing your system to work overtime.

- **Fresher is better.** Where did your "fresh food" come from? Fresh food starts to lose nutrients when it is harvested. It is usually at least five days old before it arrives in the grocery store. The fresher the food, the better it is.

- **Go organic.** Is the food organic? Has it been sprayed with chemicals or fertilized with chemicals that are toxic to you?

In a perfect nutritional world, you would grow your own organic food, harvest just enough to meet your immediate needs and eat it raw. However, this is not very practical for most people.

I can help you gain the knowledge of what is good, better and best. It requires taking responsibility for what you put in your body.

I suggest an eighty-percent raw, plant-based lifestyle that includes eight to ten fruits and vegetables every day. This includes lots of leafy greens, legumes, nuts, seeds, grains and herbs.

Your new lifestyle should include good fats, such as olive oil, coconut oil and flax. Drink two to four liters of water between meals. As you put the proper building blocks of nutrients and enzymes from food and herbs into your body, you will start on the road to a long healthy life.

Heal. Conventional medicine typically treats your symptoms with a pill for every illness. However, when you nourish your body with the proper nutrients, it can heal itself.

Nutrition is your primary disease prevention strategy. Nutrients in large enough doses can help your body heal and give it tools to fight disease. Your body wants to be healthy—when it has the proper nutrients, it will develop powerful defenses and start to heal itself.

Boost your health with large doses of herbs that can kill viruses and bacteria. Herbs will give you self-reliance and prepare you to take control of your own health needs and those of your family.

There are hundreds of herbs—many target specific areas of the body. Cayenne, garlic, ginger and onion are known as "super" herbs because they are *synergistic.* This means they increase the potency of other herbs and help the body heal in several areas. You can generally find them anywhere. I would like to share with you some of the things that I have learned about these herbs through my studies and experiences as a coach and a family nutritional herbalist.

Cayenne. Cayenne is an amazing herb with many varieties all over the world. It comes from the fruit of the red pepper plant. Legend says that Columbus discovered the pepper growing on an island off French Guiana called Devil's Island. For many years, cayenne has been used as a culinary and medicinal herb. It contains many nutrients, including alpha-tocopherois, vitamin C, vitamin A, sulfur, iron, calcium, magnesium and phosphorus, making it a great treatment for many ailments. It is a catalyst that increases the efficiency of other herbs and should be used in its powdered form.

As one of the most effective stimulants, cayenne primarily targets the digestive and circulatory systems. One teaspoon of cayenne in a glass of water taken daily will strengthen your heart. It feeds the cell structure, helping the arteries, veins and capillaries regain elasticity, while increasing and maintaining the overall health of the circulatory system. It is considered to be one of the best herbs to use in emergencies or crises because it regulates the circulatory system, boosting energy and easing the effects of stress on the body. You can use cayenne to stop bleeding or a heart attack, kill germs, stop pain and keep the body from going into shock.

One Sunday afternoon, my daughter was in the kitchen preparing dinner. She was slicing an avocado and sliced two of her fingers almost to the bone. She was squeezing her fingers tight to stop the bleeding—every time she released the pressure, blood would run down her fingers and cover her hand. I gave her one teaspoon of cayenne in one-half cup of water to drink and waited a couple of minutes. She released the pressure, and the bleeding had slowed. A few minutes later, it stopped completely.

Garlic. Garlic is known by medical professionals and scientists as a great antibiotic and fungicide. An Egyptian medical papyrus listed several garlic-based formulas for such ailments as headaches, throat problems, weakness and fatigue. In 77 AD, Roman naturalist Pliny the Elder wrote of the healing power of the garlic plant in his encyclopedia *Naturalist Historia*. He recommended garlic for poisonous bites, parasites and asthma. He listed 61 diseases that respond to garlic.

Modern medicine and science have validated the use and effectiveness of garlic as a medicinal herb. In 1858, Louis Pasteur first recognized garlic for its antibacterial properties. Since that time, garlic has been used very effectively on both internal and external infections.

Garlic is a source of iron, calcium, silicon, sulfur, copper, zinc, chromium, selenium, vitamin A, vitamin B_1 and vitamin C. Fresh garlic, powdered garlic and garlic oil will give you the power to stop or prevent most types of infection internally or externally. Garlic oil applied externally or fresh garlic taken internally will take care of earaches, sore throats, congestion and much more. These ailments would usually send you running to the doctor. Now, you can take care of them yourself.

Ginger. Ginger is native to the coast of India and is most commonly used by the food industry as a spice to flavor different foods. It is a source of iron, sodium, silicon, manganese, phosphorus, chromium, vitamin A, vitamin B_2, B_3, B_{12}, vitamin C and biotin.

Ginger has been used in Chinese medicine for centuries as a remedy for digestive problems, fever, coughing, nausea, diarrhea and rheumatism. Studies have also shown that ginger's anti-nausea properties can be used to control motion sickness better than over-the-counter and prescription drugs—without the side affects.

Ginger stimulates the circulatory system, thereby increasing fluids circulating through the body. These fluids will bring nourishment and carry off poisons as they flush inflamed joints, tendons, a feverish body or a clogged wheezy chest. Increased circulation helps to open all of the elimination channels and effectively restore well-being.

Onions. Onions were one of the first plants to be cultivated and can be found all over the world. They have been used for centuries to treat such ailments as arthritis, asthma, colds, influenza and rheumatism and are an exceptional antiseptic. Research directed by Dr. Victor Gurewich, director of the vascular laboratory at St. Elizabeth's Hospital, Boston, Massachusetts, shows that onions cleanse the blood, lower high blood pressure and help break up fluid congestion.

Reach for an onion and apply it externally or take it internally fresh or in capsule form as an antidote for insect bites, earaches, or any badly bruised, jammed or sprained body part.

Last winter, my husband and I were to attend a convention. My husband was feeling run down. By the time we flew in and got to the hotel, he was congested and feeling miserable. I went to the store and bought an onion and garlic. I sliced up the onion, made a poultice by warming the onion until it was slimy, wrapped it in cheesecloth and put it on his chest for the night. I then chopped up the garlic, mixed it with olive oil and applied it to his feet. In the morning, he was amazed at how good he felt. We were able to attend and enjoy the convention.

Additional Food Tips

• Steak only has 5.4 grams of protein per 100 calories—broccoli has 11.2 grams, almost twice as much.

• Milk has 194 mg of calcium per 100 calories, romaine lettuce has 257 mg, kale has 455 mg, and bok choy has 1,055 mg.

- Peppermint is soothing and relaxing to the nerves and was found to block headache pain by researchers at the University of Kiel.

- Lavender has the ability to promote tissue regeneration and speed wound healing as discovered by the French scientist Rene Gattefosse.

- Comfrey is a potent cell "proliferant," which means that it actively promotes the growth of new cells in all body tissue.

- Broccoli is a super-food due to its high level of phytochemicals and their potential to mobilize the body's natural disease-fighting resources.

- Greens are the most nutrient dense foods that we have available according to Michael Liebman, PhD, professor of human nutrition at the University of Wyoming. Greens can help control blood pressure, reduce the risk of heart disease, reduce the risk of cancer and protect against vision loss.

- Elderflower and licorice are two herbs that have immune-stimulating capabilities.

Be Healthy, Feel Healthy, Live Healthy

This journey to health is about discovery—the discovery of what feeds you, what nourishes you, what helps your body heal, and what makes your life feel extraordinary. Thinking differently about your nutrition and health may seem like a big task. Just take one step at a time. Start when you get up in the morning by drinking fresh water. After a few days, add a pinch of cayenne to your water or to fresh juice and see how you feel. It will start you off on the right foot and get those unwanted toxins out of your body.

You can do this! You are created by the choices you make each day. As you boost your nutrition with nutrient-dense foods and healing herbs that support your body, you will find your extraordinary life.

You will find it helpful to hire a health coach or nutritional herbalist to support you through your journey. Together, make a plan that will give your body only those foods that will build and honor your body, and step into the greatest health independence you have ever had. Have a great journey.

DEBRA LIDDELL, CDC, CFH, CNH
Speaker, Coach, Herbal Nutritionist

It is not about just living . . .
It is about living with health and passion

(541) 647-7630
debbie@theherbalnutritionist.com
www.theherbalnutritionist.com

Love of life, a sincere interest in people and a desire to share her passion for helping others are the defining points of Debra's work. She brings thirty years of experience in teaching and counseling and has a background in child development and family relations. She has also raised five successful children of her own and is blessed with eighteen grandchildren.

Debra is a Certified Dream Coach® as well as a Certified Family and Nutritional Herbalist. Her passion is to help others feel their best and live their dreams with incredible health and vitality. She believes that daily choices directly affect our well-being and that health and success are interconnected. She takes the mystery out of healthy living and provides understanding of what the body needs to live a full life.

Debra gives fun, fact-filled presentations that empower participants with the knowledge that allows them to feel fabulous and pursue their dreams. She offers realistic tips, goals and ideas that encourage a long, high-quality life. Debra also provides continued support, through one-on-one coaching, for those who are truly committed to living a healthy and successful life.

Five Ps to Make Life-Enhancing Changes

By Jackie Roberge

Why do we often wait until we are faced with a life-threatening diagnosis before we make changes and create the life we so long for? The simple answer is that it is easier not to change, even though most life changes result in a more positive experience.

Sometimes, change can be disruptive and unsettling. As a life purpose coach, I help facilitate change, so it is experienced as stimulating and energizing! My main focus is working with cancer patients. In this chapter, I will share some interesting insights about why cancer patients are receptive to making big changes and what we can learn from them. I will also provide you with a greater understanding of the dynamics of change, as well as exercises you can do to help you move from contemplating change to enabling life-enhancing changes now.

To set the stage for making change, it is useful to look at the relationship between your ego and your soul. The ego is the part of you that establishes and identifies you as an individual. A big part of your ego's role is to keep you safe, comfortable, healthy and reasonably happy. The basis for resistance to change comes from your ego. Change that moves you out of your comfort zone can feel threatening to your ego.

Your soul, or your Higher Self, is the part of you that is eternal. It has your higher good and your spiritual growth and development as its focus. Your soul wants you to be fulfilled and live your life purpose—that which you came into this world to do and which is most fulfilling for you. Your soul is constantly guiding you and exposing you to situations and challenges that help you grow and move you towards your purpose. As you make decisions in life, you are unconsciously being guided by either your soul or your ego. Once you are aware of the ego-soul dynamic, it is easier to consciously create harmony between your inner guides and facilitate positive change.

I will take you through a process I created called *The Five Ps to Make Life-Enhancing Changes* now. As we move through the steps, I will show you ways to listen to your soul and ensure buy-in from the ego, so change can be viewed as positive, and an internal alignment is attained between ego and soul.

I recommend you use a journal to capture your thoughts and insights as they arise. Reviewing them later, you may be surprised at the gems you have recorded and forgotten.

The Five Ps

1. Pain Point: Identify Your Emotional Pain Point. Pain, both physical and emotional, is a strong motivator for change. In the case of cancer patients, the diagnosis triggers fear and other emotional pain, and the disease itself can bring physical pain. Clearly, the motivation to change in order to become healthy again is very high.

> *"Not until the pain of the same is greater than the pain of change will you embrace change."*
> —Dave Ramsey, American financial advisor,
> radio host and speaker

In your life, if part of you is satisfied or comfortable enough where you are, you may not be ready to risk trading comfort for a potentially destabilizing outcome. In order to motivate yourself, you must identify a significant gap between where you are and where you long to be in some area of your life. This gap is what creates the pain point—the deep hurt you feel that is caused by your longing to create alignment. It is in feeling your pain at the heart or soul level that you will gain clarity about what you need to work on.

Your pain point may be in relation to your profession, a relationship, your body, or it could be more of a general feeling of a lack of happiness or fulfillment. The pain or gap often leads to stress, lack of alignment, inner turmoil and, if not addressed, to disease. Disease is one of the body's ways of telling you the situation needs to be dealt with urgently. Identifying and feeling your pain point may seem scary. It may feel easier to keep it hidden. However, if you are ready to feel and own it, your pain can become the key to propel you into action.

Exercise. Here is an exercise to help you identify the deep, heartfelt pain in your life, which may be different from what you think it is. Give yourself about one hour of quiet time to do this exercise. Get a journal or a notepad. Find a comfortable, quiet place and center yourself with a few deep breaths.

On the top of a page in your journal, write, "The deep pain I am experiencing right now is . . ." and start writing about a specific issue in your life. Use bullet points or short sentences. Write down what comes up without censoring anything. Your soul knows the pain. If you simply listen quietly and write what comes up, you will be able to tap into your inner wisdom. Keep experimenting with different ways of expressing your pain point until what you write elicits a strong emotional reaction and, possibly, even some tears. Only then have you tuned into your soul and felt the pain that will inspire change.

For example, your first statement may read, "The deep pain I am experiencing right now is the unhappiness in my long-term relationship." The last statement you write may look something like, "I don't feel loved or lovable. I don't know how to truly love myself." These last statements reflect your underlying or deep-felt pain—the pain that needs your attention.

Once you have your pain point, take a few more deep breaths and then identify what you long for. Write at the top of another page, "What I long for is . . ." and then begin writing what that is. For example, "I long to love myself and show myself love every day," or "I long to feel truly connected with my spouse and feel loved and accepted just the way I am."

2. Power: Ignite Your Inner Power. To make important changes in your life, you need to feel both your pain and your power. Empowerment is one of the most important steps on the road to living a more fulfilled life. The kind of power I am referring to does not come from money or a big title. It comes from taking ownership of your pain and for where you are in your life right now and then choosing to do something about it. For cancer patients, the power comes when they become conscious that taking ownership of their circumstance translates into the power to change the situation and facilitate healing.

When you feel angry and blame others for your pain, you are unconsciously giving your power to others. Once you stand up and say, "I am responsible for my pain," you open the door to more confidence, to the courage to create change and to claim the life you really want and deserve!

Exercise. Write down all the ways you can think of that you may have contributed to your pain. Continuing the example from the previous exercise about pain in a long-term relationship, you might write, "I did not appreciate my own strengths. I let other people's opinions count more than mine. I did not give myself enough room to be me within my relationship. I did not ask for what I really wanted."

Once you have a list, read it over and take responsibility for your part in it. If the urge arises to blame others or situations in your past, stop and take a deep breath. Know that when you blame others, you give away your power. Acceptance and ownership put you in the driver's seat. Keep in mind, there are no mistakes in life, only opportunities to learn and grow. In order to learn and really benefit from past challenges, you need to take action that moves you in a new and positive direction.

At this point in the exercise, I invite you to give yourself a hug—literally, a real, loving hug. Let yourself feel compassion, knowing that you did your best, and you can now support yourself in a new, more loving and reinforcing way. The good news is that the statements you wrote down are things over which you have control.

Now, reframe all the statements you wrote in positive, present tense. For example, "I appreciate and recognize my own strengths. I value my own opinions. I am at ease being my true self. I am clear on what I want and ask for it in a firm, yet loving, way."

If any of these statements are hard to say, they are the ones you should focus on and practice every day. Write them all down and repeat them as positive, daily affirmations. Don't just read them—allow yourself to feel your energy shift and revel in the feeling of how joyful it is to experience each one.

"Whatever we plant in our subconscious mind and nourish with repetition and emotion will one day become a reality."
—Earl Nightingale, American motivational writer and author

3. Permission: Give Yourself Permission. After identifying your emotional pain point and igniting your inner power, you can now identify what you need to dissolve your pain and move toward that list of things you long for (the last part of the pain point exercise). This is when you may need to give yourself permission in order to move ahead with life-enhancing changes. Remember, your ego wants to keep you safe and comfortable. Making changes threatens the status quo, so it is important to get buy-in from your ego. Having inner permission and alignment creates readiness for change.

For cancer patients, the situation is quite different because the ego actually feels threatened by the status quo due to the cancer. It no longer feels comfortable and safe. This is why change, even big change, is often easier to implement for a cancer patient since the ego views change as a necessary part of the solution.

Exercise. On a new sheet of paper, create three vertical columns. On the top of the left column, write *Next Steps*. On the top of the middle column, write *Ego Fears*. On the top of the right column, write *Support*.

Begin to fill out the columns. Continuing with our relationship example, in the *Next Steps* column, you would write the immediate next step to move towards what you long for. For example, "Talk to my partner about my pain." In the next column, write down concerns or fears your ego may have. For example, "My partner may not accept me and might get angry. I won't be able to express myself well." In the third column, write down what your ego needs in order to feel safe moving ahead with this step. For example, "Practice what I'm going to say ahead of time," or "Express the pain in the presence of a therapist who can support us."

Once you have suggestions from your ego, you can commit to the ones you are comfortable with. Keeping your commitments is key to maintaining the support of your ego. Remember, your ego really does want you to be happy—it just sometimes has biases and often thinks short term. Keep in mind, the ego also has insights and ideas in terms of increasing the safety and comfort level of change because keeping you safe is its main job! Please resist the temptation to ignore or plough through your fears. Instead, I invite you to tap into the voice of the ego and do internal brainstorming to see how you can create readiness for change.

Continue to write down your next steps, fears and the support you need to move towards your new reality. Try to deal with one step at a time, so you develop confidence and do not get overwhelmed.

4. Passion: Experience Your Passion. When you anchor into the childlike energy of your passion and experience the drive it generates for you to move courageously forward, there is no end to what you can achieve. I have observed that cancer *thrivers*—survivors who feel that their lives are better since having cancer—have something in common. Along their journey from pain to fulfillment, they found something that they became very excited about—something that moved them so deeply, it flooded them with energy and propelled them forward to share their newfound passion with others.

As you move through the Five Ps, be on the lookout for something you may want to share with the world. Again, continuing with our example, as you practice expressing your feelings and needs and really loving yourself, you may feel inspired to write about your experiences. Writing might start as a blog and then lead to a book. You may want to take courses to become an expert in the field of self-love and give public lectures or host workshops. Alternatively, you may decide that volunteer work helping children develop self-love is the most meaningful way to express your passion and find fulfillment.

Discovering your passion is really about finding the blessing in the darkness of your struggle. If you are hiding from or denying your pain, you may be missing an opportunity to discover a deep-felt passion that could lead to life-enhancing changes you would never have thought possible.

> *"The cave you fear to enter holds the treasure you seek."*
> —Joseph Campbell, American mythologist, writer and lecturer

Remember, your soul is constantly guiding you and leading you to situations and experiences that are essential for you to grow and prosper. Being watchful for hidden blessings can help you see the journey in a new light. Change does not have to be a struggle—the journey can be fun and exhilarating! With this shift in perspective, you can go into any challenging situation expecting to find a blessing and having faith that everything on your path is there for your benefit and may hold the key to increased growth and fulfillment.

5. Purpose: Live with Purpose, Flow and Fulfillment. We all have a deep desire to make a meaningful contribution in life. Living a purposeful life leads to true and lasting fulfillment and flow in everyday life. Being in *flow* means that the people, ideas and teachers you need show up right when you need them. When I help cancer patients find their purpose and see them share their passion with a sense of alignment and inner harmony, I know they have been healed at a deep level, beyond physical healing.

Following your passion often leads you to your purpose. However, there is an opportunity to understand and live your purpose at a much more meaningful level. This includes knowing the details of the transformation you are designed to make, with whom you are meant to work and what state they are in when you are finished helping them. What I am describing is part of the True Purpose™ methodology developed by Tim Kelley, author of the book *True Purpose: 12 Strategies for Discovering the Difference You Are Meant to Make*, Transcendent Solutions Press, 2009. Getting clarity around your purpose is inspiring and allows you to move forward more quickly and with confidence. If this is of interest to you, I encourage you to find a trained True Purpose coach who can lead you through the process and help you accelerate your journey on the path to flow and fulfillment.

Experiencing the Five Ps

Now that you are equipped with a greater understanding of the dynamic relationship between your ego and your soul, you no longer have to wait to make meaningful changes in your life. You can give yourself the power and permission to create the circumstances that facilitate deep and lasting changes and, ultimately, greater fulfillment now. An essential step is to give yourself the time to slow down and go through the steps, reflecting on where you are and where you long to be. Do not put this off. You deserve to be happy, prosperous and fulfilled! If you did not have time to do the exercises as you read them, schedule time in your agenda when you can complete them. Dedicating time to reflection and inner work is a necessary component for creating change.

I invite you to let your heart guide you on your journey and use the Five Ps to help you move confidently ahead. If you get stuck or need encouragement along the way, find someone who can support you—a coach, a friend or a family member. Remember to be open to finding the hidden blessing along the way and experiencing a joyful, uplifting transformational journey.

JACKIE ROBERGE
True Purpose™ Coach, Cancershift
Coach, Speaker, Workshop Leader,
Yoga and Meditation Teacher

*Helping women face their fears, feel their power
and discover their passion!*

(514) 931-9670
Jackie@cancershift.com
www.cancershift.com

J ackie is a passionate life purpose coach and a dynamic speaker, workshop leader and writer. Her approach is infused with spiritual insights, joy and compassion. She is intuitive, strategic and creative as she helps people open up to their inner guidance, so they are able to live with more joy, passion and purpose.

Through her work with cancer clients, Jackie has developed a strong conviction about the importance of a holistic approach to healing. She empowers her clients to discover the meaning of, and actively participate in, their own healing journey. The result is inner harmony, self-love and deep healing.

Before beginning her career as a coach, Jackie studied business at Queen's University in Kingston, Ontario, and worked in marketing and as a consultant for more than twenty years. During this time, she discovered the power of meditation and yoga to help reduce stress and create a more peaceful and balanced life. She now teaches these modalities to others. Jackie lives in Montreal, Quebec, with her husband and their two daughters. She has a passion for spirituality, sports, laughter and healthy living.

Looking Within to Discover the Real You

Reshape Your Self-Image from the Inside Out

By Tammikka Lynn Chambers

Your journey to a healthy, positive self-image can begin today— no matter where you are!

Your self-image development began in your childhood and has been shaped over the years through your heritage, society, culture and life experiences. Self-image is based on an internal picture of yourself, consciously and subconsciously. It has a major impact on your successes and failures. It is also based on character. Recognizing your integrity and honesty relative to your values is essential for a positive self-image.

In this chapter, we will discover how your self-image impacts your life journey. I will offer tools to help you discover the real you and reshape your self-image. This will lead to a healthy, restored and peaceful you. It is the path to creating the life and relationships you want!

> *"An individual's self-concept is the core of his personality.*
> *It affects every aspect of human behavior. A strong, positive*
> *self-image is the best possible preparation for success."*
> —Dr. Joyce Brothers, American psychologist

My Journey Is Everyone's Journey

My journey to a healthy self-image began during my early childhood years. My self-image was framed around believing I was smart, intelligent and beautiful. My parents instilled a core value system that focused on working hard, sacrificing for those you love, giving one hundred and ten percent in all situations and pursuing your dreams. Achieving goals was accomplished by applying strong work habits and discipline.

One spring day in the ninth grade, my life drastically changed when someone I thought was my friend took something very precious and valuable from me. Suddenly, I viewed myself as unintelligent, unworthy, naïve, irresponsible and unattractive. The experience produced feelings of rejection, low self-worth and lack of trust. I went from loving life and chasing dreams to wondering why I even existed. It took many years to understand the true impact of how that event influenced my life and deterred me from fulfilling my life purpose and dreams.

For several years following this incident, my self-image was formed by my personal relationships. I was constantly looking for validation from others. I made many decisions to please other people without taking myself into consideration. My self-image significantly changed from believing in myself as someone with great merit to looking for approval, value and worth from others. When your self-image is shaped around what other people think, you slowly lose your self-identity. You can become so afraid of being rejected by people that you are willing to forsake discovering the true essence of who you are.

My journey to reshaping my self-image started about ten years ago when I decided that my ninth grade experience would no longer have any power over how I defined and viewed myself. I finally realized that until I cared for and loved myself, I would be unable to care for and love others. First, I had to take a closer look at exactly what self-image was and its different elements.

You may not have suffered the same challenges or situations as I have. Despite the different paths traveled by each person, my story of re-discovering my self-image can show you the way.

What Is Self-Image?

Self-image is how you see yourself. This includes how you hold and understand your abilities, personality, strengths, weaknesses and physical appearance. Self-image can be described through this simple acronym:

- **Status** you feel you have

- **Evaluation** of your strengths and weaknesses

- **Loving** yourself

- **Feelings** about what others believe and think about you

Through the journey of reshaping my self-image, I discovered three different, yet integral, components. Each plays a distinct role in reshaping your self-image.

How others see you. This fundamental is built on another's opinion based on an encounter they have with you. People observe your behaviors and form an opinion without your input. From this observation, they can see you in a positive light or a negative light.

For example, someone may be seen at work as being unfriendly or unhappy because they rarely smile. Perhaps that person is simply focused and intensely dedicated.

How you *perceive* others view you. The second component of self-image is based on perception. This is when we create our understanding by organizing and interpreting sensory information. Perception is subjective, open to interpretation and can yield false conclusions. You can never fully understand another person's perception because it is seen through their thoughts and eyes only.

For example, you may think someone disapproves of the way that you dress by how you perceive they look at you. However, you later discover that they were simply observing how you put your clothes together because they, in fact, admired it and wanted to learn from it. It is always best to avoid making assumptions on how others may view you.

How you see yourself. This is the most important arena of self-image. It revolves around the personal opinions and beliefs you have about yourself—both positive and negative. Your opinions and beliefs are formed by your upbringing—your family life, your heritage, your society and your life experiences. This is the area you have the greatest influence over and what will shape you into being the person you most want to be in life.

> *"Never allow anyone to change who you are because you will never be happy in who they will have you to be."*
> —Janis Clark, African-American beauty stylist

Why Is Your Self-Image Important?

Understanding self-image is critical to the journey of reshaping yourself. The way you feel about yourself affects the way you project yourself to others. Relationships and daily interactions are influenced by your self-image. There are three important reasons why self-image is so vitally important.

It deepens your structural foundation. Your self-image frames your structural foundation. It is built on your mindset from which come the basic principles and belief systems that govern your life. Your thoughts have a significant impact on your inner self and how you view yourself. Your strength, power and longevity are determined by your foundation. You can only go as high and far as your structural foundation will support you. However, only you truly know how deep your foundation extends. The depth of your structural foundation will be tested during trials and challenging times.

It determines your success in life. A healthy self-image generates productivity and success in life. It propels you to set goals, make sound decisions and soar in your personal and professional life. It helps you accomplish significant achievements and milestones along your journey and provides an inner strength that compels you to never quit. Your attitude will be focused on positive thoughts. This is where your attitude determines your altitude and success level in life. You will take responsibility for your actions and be motivated to be proactive and responsive.

It develops your best self. Your self-image motivates you to discover the best in yourself and embrace your unique qualities and characteristics. You will cherish your individuality and love the fact that there is only one you. You are uniquely designed and created. No matter what others tell you or what you experience, *you* are valuable, and your uniqueness is your best quality.

> *"To be yourself in a world that is constantly trying to make you something else is the greatest accomplishment."*
> —Ralph Waldo Emerson, American writer

Successful Keys on How to Reshape Your Self-Image

Your self-image can be reshaped by the following five keys, regardless of life situations, circumstances or relationships. Please recognize and understand that the only person who has the power to remain consistent in all situations is you.

Key One: Dedicate yourself to self-love and respect. This is the first important step. Stay faithful to your essence and do not compromise who you are. Get in touch with your true self and harmonize your beliefs and actions with the person you really are. Generating self-love and respect is based on loving yourself, which will allow you to love others. It is important to establish a standard for yourself and refuse to compromise with how you allow people to treat you, including loved ones. Until you love yourself genuinely, you will be unable to love others authentically.

When you set a higher standard of living, you give yourself permission to raise the bar and proclaim that you want the best for yourself. We live in a society where many imitate what they see around them. The good side of this is that when others see how you love and respect yourself, it can inspire them to do the same.

Key Two: Dispel negative thoughts and opinions. The next important key is to identify the negative ideas and thoughts that prevent you from embracing and loving your true essence. Every negative opinion must be replaced by a positive, healthy thought. Toxic thoughts block you from accomplishing your goals, dreams and life aspirations.

You have the power within you to redefine your self-image and not allow negativity to continue to play a significant role in your life. This helps rebuild your belief system. It took many years to create your current belief system based on negative thoughts. You must stay true to the process of creating your new belief system. As you capture new positive thoughts, you will begin to love yourself enough to know that those healthy thoughts are vital to your success in order to reshape a positive self-image. (For more information on beliefs, see Beverly Lenz's chapter, "CPR for Your Soul" on page 11.)

Key Three: Deliver daily declarations to create a new mindset. The third valuable key is activating your visions and dreams by speaking positive declarations to reinforce what you believe about yourself. Declarations are formal affirmations, professions or statements. Speaking the words aloud will support you by hearing yourself state the new truth of what is so. The way you think creates your reality for yourself.

I encourage you to say your declarations daily and make them an active part of your life. Your self-image centers on your mindset, which is based on your belief system. It is demonstrated through your attitude. There must be alignment between what is in your heart and what is spoken. Your mindset transformation is connected to what you say. Saying your declarations can transport your self-image to new levels, regardless of how your current situation appears.

Here are some suggestions for declarations.

• I was created as a designer's original, never to be duplicated.

• I love myself because I am fearfully and wonderfully made!

• I forgive myself for past mistakes, and I focus on being a better me.

• I walk in power and love and have a well-balanced mind.

• I will not settle for anything less than my destiny because there is great purpose in me.

- I have the creative ability to produce good works, and I am empowered to prosper, flourish and thrive.

- Today, unexpected favor goes before me while goodness and mercy follow me all the days of my life!

Make the decision to deliberately meditate on things that are true, noble, reputable, authentic, compelling and gracious. Claim the best and the beautiful. Discover things to celebrate. Meditation births declaration; declaration births beliefs; beliefs birth a new mindset and life perspective.

> *"It's repetition of affirmations that leads to belief. And once that belief becomes a deep conviction, things will begin to happen."*
> —Muhammad Ali, African-American world champion boxer

Key Four: Discover your life purpose. Discovering your purpose for living in the world is vital to reshaping your self-image. The fact that you were born means you have contributions to make. You have the ability to influence lives in a positive manner.

Identify your gifts, talents and skills. Many things you enjoy and excel in yield positive results and contentment for you. Know your strengths as well as your vulnerabilities and weaknesses. Your strengths can become an open door of opportunity. Being mindful of your weaknesses enables you to build upon them and not have them be a hindrance to the pursuit of your goals.

Start designing your purpose by writing a list of the things that bring you joy and the things for which you are acknowledged. From the list, you can formulate ideas that create a beneficial hobby or business. When you discover your purpose, you bring significance to your life. Knowing and taking steps towards your purpose can reshape your self-image because it moves you in the direction of your greatest strengths.

(For more information on purpose, see Jackie Roberge's chapter, "Five Ps to Make Life-Enhancing Changes" on page 111.)

Key Five: Develop the good in life. Developing the good in life comes from actively practicing the first four keys. Through your dedication to self-respect, dispelling negative thoughts, delivering daily declarations and discovering your life purpose, you will develop a clear vision for your life. That vision will ignite the passion to love and to cherish yourself at all times, creating an optimal life.

> *"This is my life. It is my one time to be me.*
> *I want to experience every good thing."*
> —Maya Angelou, African-American poet

Benefits of Reshaping Your Self-Image

Through the journey of reshaping your self-image, you will begin to see the results from the keys you have activated in your life. You will see positive changes in how you view yourself and what you believe about yourself. These changes will influence your decisions, relationships and your outlook on life in the following ways.

Heartfelt, wise decisions. Your decisions will be heartfelt and wise because they will be built on a sound foundation, healthy mindset and your reformed belief system that is now founded on optimistic thoughts and a positive outlook on life. A useful technique is writing down various solutions to a problem and listing the pros and cons for each proposed solution. This will help you carefully weigh options and make an intelligent decision.

Your decisions will be focused on improving and enhancing your life for the better and will not compromise your true essence or your belief system. One of the greatest indicators for ensuring you are making sound decisions for yourself is to allow peace to rule over your heart and mind with the decision.

Healthy relationships. During your journey of reshaping your self-image, healthy relationships will emerge and develop. People around you will become part of the transformation process. Your relationships will naturally evolve because you now see yourself differently. You live life with an optimistic attitude and have a belief system based on a healthy mindset. This will be new for those around you because your actions, responses, attitudes and conversations will be different.

You will have a new level of confidence in your abilities and live life full of purpose. Your relationships will be based on truth, integrity and a high standard of living. Those who really love you will embrace the restored you and encourage you to believe the best in yourself and not compromise yourself for anyone or anything.

Joy beyond happiness. Your new self-image will allow you to have joy and passion for life. Living life at the joy level is a step beyond happiness because happiness is based on the happenings in your life. When good things occur, you are happy. When tragic events occur, you are not happy. Joy, on the other hand, is a positive attitude or pleasant emotion that rises above situations and circumstances. This joy can last during all the seasons of your life.

A healthy self-image will allow you to pursue life with joy—no matter what is happening. You will have an optimistic attitude toward every situation that comes your way. You will believe negative situations are temporary and will start working toward a response to improve the circumstances.

Always believe that you were born to win, and you have the inner power, strength and ability to overcome. You can fulfill your life purpose and dreams while living a peaceful life. You cannot change events and circumstances. However, you can control and change your response to those same events and circumstances.

The journey to discovering a healthy self-image is an invaluable process and experience. You can love yourself from the inside out—especially your reshaped self-image. Believe the best in yourself and continue to build upon your solid structural foundation. Embrace your uniqueness and all your distinctive qualities and characteristics. Continue to renew your mindset. Focus on striving to be the best you, for no one can beat you at that!

TAMMIKKA LYNN CHAMBERS
Licensed Minister,
Motivational Speaker, Teacher

(510) 932-2953
Tammikka@TLChambersEmpowers.com
www.TLChambersEmpowers.com

Tammikka has transitioned from a successful corporate leader to an entrepreneur, author, workshop leader and motivational speaker. As a licensed minister, she has answered the call to her true life purpose, which is to educate, empower and equip individuals to create vision and achieve their purpose and dreams. Her heart's desire is to see each person she meets fulfill their destiny and leave a legacy for the next generation.

Her personal journey of reshaping and transforming her own life to a life of hope, faith and purpose truly inspires and encourage others. With a unique teaching gift that allows Tammikka to share life-changing spiritual techniques, she helps individuals discover they can overcome any situation. She has a mission in life to help people build a healthy, whole, prosperous tomorrow—starting today.

Tammikka is an established finance professional and has facilitated many workshops and seminars in the San Francisco Bay Area on various topics, including practical life principles and financial stewardship techniques. She is passionate about making a positive impact in the community and changing lives. Tammikka enjoys traveling, reading, mentoring young women and spending time with her beautiful nieces.

Journaling at the Heart of Changing Your Life

By Janet Wiszowaty

In today's world of technology, it can be difficult to focus on what is really important in life. The media would like you to believe that having a new house with the most up-to-date appliances will make you happy, or that a BMW convertible will make you look successful. However, you have something much more valuable. You have an inner knowing that can be tapped into at any point and when you find that source, you are able to quiet the outside noise and make the decisions that are right for you. This chapter is about using journaling as a tool to connect within and guide you to a healthier and happier life.

When you were young, you may have been given your first journal, or diary, as they were often then called. If you had a large birthday party, you may have even received more than one diary! Perhaps you could hardly wait for everyone to leave, so you could start writing down all your secrets. As you grew older, writing in your journal likely became less important. Why was that? Was it because you had a busy life? Were you afraid that someone might find it and read it? Perhaps you were harassed by an older sibling about it, or you just did not think it was *cool* anymore to write down your thoughts. Whatever the reason, no matter how old you are, now is the time to pick up that journal and pen and begin to write again.

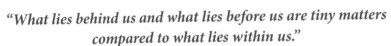

"What lies behind us and what lies before us are tiny matters compared to what lies within us."
—Ralph Waldo Emerson, American writer

Benefits of Journaling

Journaling is a process of going inside yourself and exploring what is there, hidden in the secret corners of your being. It is writing about what makes your soul sing, as well as writing about what makes you tick. Some people write poetry in their journal; some express their anger and upsets; some write about their hopes, dreams and future visions; some express through drawing or doodling as they journal. Ultimately, there is no exact way to journal. It is about your unique way of expressing your truth through the pen and paper. Basically, journaling is a conversation with your own self. Here are some of the benefits.

Getting to know yourself better. When you write and let the words pour forth from your heart, you bypass your logical mind. What shows up on the paper is whatever is true for you in the moment. There is no need to judge or be concerned what others may think. These words are just for you. Your thoughts and feelings flow through your hand and onto the paper. During times of confusion, writing can help to release information of what might be behind the confusion. New ideas and solutions can start to emerge. During times of joy, writing can help you connect with the goodness of life. Writing is a gift to yourself and a way to get to know yourself much better.

Releasing grievances and pain. We often hold on to past hurts and pain. Journaling can help reduce stress in your life by releasing pent-up frustrations that linger in your mind, affecting your mood, which, in turn, can affect your physical well-being. You can process your pain or grief by writing letters to those with whom you cannot share your truth for any reason. It may be because they have passed away.

Whatever the reason, you can use journaling as a way to release what is on your mind. You can write a letter about it, say everything you truly want to say and then let it go by burning it or tearing it up. The process is healing and cleansing and can help you forgive and move on in life.

Accessing what is most valuable to you. We often do not even know what we want until we truly ask ourselves and write it down. Journaling can help you gain clarity about the dreams and visions you have for your life. You may unearth something that would not have come to light if you had not taken the time to write it down. This can lead you in a new direction for your life that is more aligned with your deepest wish.

Discovering your progress. Periodically, you can look back at what you have written and discover all that you have learned, how you have changed and how far you have come. Your journal pages can reflect the challenges you have overcome. You may even have a great appreciation for the things you have accomplished that you have forgotten about. You will likely shed a few tears or laugh as you read about things from your past.

Suggested Writing Topics

There are many ways to journal. Here are some powerful suggestions for you to get started.

Write about your dreams and visions for your life. When you put your dreams and visions down on paper, you are taking ownership of them, claiming them and giving them life. In this way, your dreams can start to take form. Write them down as if you are already living them. Take in the smells, the sounds and the feelings of the sought-after experience. Be specific about the outcome you desire.

I personally love flying—all I have to do is close my eyes and envision being in my seat on the airplane. My seat belt is tightened, and my carry-on luggage is safely under the seat in front of me as I savor the feeling of the plane lifting off from the runway into the sky heading to an exotic destination.

What dreams and visions will you write about?

Record your night dreams. Your dreams at night can be very revealing as to what is going on in your subconscious mind. Your subconscious is the part of your mind that influences the thoughts, feelings and action of which you are not fully aware. Keeping a journal beside your bed to record your dreams can be a good resource into knowing yourself. Simply write down your dreams as you remember them. Include any sensations, emotions, people, animals or significant items that appear. Writing it down may bring you insight into what is happening in your life as it is reflected in your dreams. If you have a recurring dream, read through your previous notations to see if there are any common threads. You can also hire a dream analyst to help you understand your dream's deeper meaning.

Express your gratitude. Keeping a journal that records the things you are grateful for each day is often referred to as a gratitude journal. I have found my gratitude journal to be highly supportive in assisting me to keep a positive attitude and a higher perspective on life. Recording what you are grateful for each day is especially useful if you are challenged with negative self-talk.

One way to keep the journal is writing about what you are grateful for now on one side of the page, and what you are grateful for in the future on the other side of the page. When writing about the future, write it in the present tense, as if it is happening now. For example, you can write, "I am deeply grateful for my precious hybrid car," or "I hold immense gratitude for my amazing husband and our beautiful marriage together."

You can write your gratitudes in the morning when you wake up or at night just before you go to sleep. Even on difficult days, when you feel there is not much to be grateful for, just put your pen to paper and write down what you are grateful for anyway. You may be surprised at what you discover. There is always so much to be thankful for, including the air that we breathe.

Have a dialogue with your subconscious mind. Psychologist Carl Jung created a concept called *active imagination.* This is where you have a dialogue with parts or aspects of yourself that tend to be hidden or not as accessible to your everyday conscious mind. For instance, you may want to have a conversation with your heart and see what it has to say. Perhaps you want to dialogue with the wounded child in you. Another option is to dialogue with your Higher Self, or the part of you that already knows the best course of action to take in various situations.

You write out the dialogue as if writing a screenplay. First write your name, followed by your words. Here's an example:

• *Lisa: I would like to please speak to my Higher Self.*

• Next line is the words of the Higher Self. *Higher Self: I am here. What is it that you want to ask of me?*

• Continue with the dialogue in this fashion.

In my experience and that of many others, great wisdom and awareness pour forth from this exercise. Give it a try and discover what is revealed from the depths of your subconscious mind.

"Words are a form of action, capable of influencing change."
—Ingrid Bengis, American writer

Sharing Your Writing

Though much of journal writing is private, great power, and even healing, can take place from sharing your writing with others. I first discovered the power of shared writing in 1983. My husband and I attended a workshop where we were given a question to answer. We each had ninety minutes to respond to the question in writing. You may think that ninety minutes is a very long to time to write. However, it was not nearly enough time to fully answer the profound question we were given.

We were asked, "Why do you want to live?" My husband and I both wrote out our responses and then exchanged our journals to read each other's answer. It was a turning point in our marriage. It opened us up to a deeper understanding of ourselves and a deeper understanding of each other.

I invite you to find ways to share some of your writings. Here are some options.

Find a writing buddy. Choose someone to practice writing with and share your writing together. It can be your spouse, a friend, a co-worker or a family member. Meet regularly with them—maybe once a month or once a week. Between the two of you, pick a question or topic to write about. Give the writing a time limit. Ten minutes for one topic may be sufficient to begin with. You may choose to use a timer, clock or watch to keep you both on track. After the allotted time is completed, you can exchange notebooks to read each other's writing silently and dialogue about it afterwards.

A variation on this is to take turns reading what you wrote aloud. Though this can certainly be more vulnerable, it offers the benefit of hearing your words spoken, as well as listening to your buddy's words.

You will need a quiet, private space for the second exercise. In either process, you will learn something about the other person and quite likely something you did not know about yourself.

Write letters. Though perhaps a bit outdated with the technology of instant messaging, texts and chats, handwritten letters are a powerful form of communication. There is something special about getting an actual handwritten letter in the mailbox. My granddaughter has started writing letters to her great grandmother, and it has enriched both of their lives.

Handwritten letters can build strong bonds and is a great way to express your love and appreciation and to share parts of yourself. Think of someone you know who would love to receive a letter from you. Take the time to write to them from your heart—where you are right now, what is important to you and the influence they have in your life. Take the time to address the envelope, put a beautiful stamp on it and send it off in the mail. Love and care seep into the fabric of the written words, and the recipient may treasure it for life.

Write magazine articles or blogs. After writing for a while, you may discover certain threads that run through much of your writing. For example, you may find that you journal about the topic of forgiveness over and over. Perhaps you write about the joy of the friendships in your life or about your frustration with your country's politics. You can gather your writings on particular topics and form them into articles. The articles can then be sent to various magazines and possibly be published.

You can start out with local publications or research what magazines might be interested in your specific topic. Your regular journal entries can also be transferred to an online blog on the Internet, where others have the opportunity to read and comment on your perspective. This allows you to share your thoughts and ideas and bring other like-minded people to you. By sharing your thoughts and life observations, you can touch and encourage others to do the same.

Write a book. Your journal writing can lead you to write your own book or ebook. For example, your journal writing about your own journey to better health can be developed into a book on self-healing. If you keep a travel journal, you can write a book about your travels. Some people are not able to travel—you will help them see, through your eyes, the exotic and wonderful places you have been. Think of the success of the book *Eat, Pray, Love* by Elizabeth Gilbert, published by Penguin Group in 2006. She inspired millions by writing about her insights while traveling through Italy, India and Bali. There are many topics covered in books and memoirs. What might be the title of your next book?

As we have explored, journal writing can facilitate personal growth, facilitate problem solving, enhance creativity, create clearer communications and understanding with others and help you write your life story. These suggestions merely touch on some of the ways you can utilize your writing to bring about change. Explore. Have fun with it. Change your life and the lives of others. Remember—there is not a right or wrong way to journal—there is only *your* way. Go get a notebook or journal and begin! Who knows where it will lead you.

JANET WISZOWATY
Speaker, Coach, Writer,
Workshop Leader

(780) 634-0775
janet@familyconnekt.com
www.familyconnekt.com
www.familyconnekt.com/blog

J anet Wiszowaty is the creator and CEO of FamilyConnekt™. According to her philosophy, life is a team sport, and we are a human family. When we all work together, miracles happen. As a certified Dream Coach®, FISH! facilitator and facilitator of Jack Canfield's Success Principles™, Janet dedicates herself to connecting individuals to their higher purpose, so they can share their greatness with the world.

During her expansive career as an emergency dispatcher with the Royal Canadian Mounted Police (RCMP), she became an expert in crisis management. Married to a now-retired RCMP officer since 1972, she raised two children while navigating through the waters of life. Moving every few years and living in four Canadian provinces in both urban and isolated communities allowed her to stretch herself and see the need for people to be connected. She discovered how one person can change the life of another forever.

As a visionary, Janet facilitates her colleagues and clients through her coaching, writing, workshops and speaking engagements—locally and internationally. Through these venues, Janet helps build connections that build strong communities.

The Power of Forgiveness Using Ancient Hawaiian Wisdom

By Yvonne Ohumukini Urness, CHSP

I t is no coincidence that you are reading these words and searching for information on power and change. There is a shift happening in the world right now and it is likely that you feel it. It is calling to you to step up. It is reminding you of who you are. It is likely one of the reasons you are reading this book.

The question many people ask is, "How do I respond to this call?" I say to them, "With love." Hawaiians use the word *aloha*. It means love. Like so many other Hawaiian words and phrases, *aloha* has many layers of meaning and expression. The root of the word consists of *alo*, which means *to be with* or *to be present*, and *oha*, which means *joy*. So, *aloha* can be translated as *being in the present with joy*.

It is easy to live with *aloha* or love when everything is going well, and the ebb and flow of life are in perfect harmony. However, what if you are experiencing frustration, anger, pain or resentment? How do you respond with love when someone has hurt you deeply, injured someone close to you or caused great despair?

The answer is still the same. Respond with love.

"He kēhau ho'oma'ema'e ke aloha."
"Love is like a cleansing dew."
—Ancient Hawaiian proverb

Holding On and Holding In

When you hold on to past hurt, pain and disappointment, you give it power over your present situation. It is like a weed that grows in your lush and verdant garden of life. It can try to disguise itself by creating a blossom in an effort to seem as though it belongs in your garden, or it can be a prickly, nasty eyesore. Either way, the more energy you give that hurt, pain and disappointment, the deeper the root grows. The deeper that root, the more damage the weed can inflict on the healthy and vibrant growth in your life.

Each time you recall the incident or action that caused the pain, you bring it to life once again in your conscious mind. You also bring to life all of the emotions associated with it, as well as all of the physiological manifestations that go along with those emotions. The manifestations can range from a short shift in mood to deep and severe depression or illness.

If this sounds familiar, you are not alone. We are all affected by our past—the good, the bad and the ugly. The past actually helps shape us into who we are today. It also provides experiences to help us avoid mistakes in our future. There is tremendous value in our past. The problems arise when we allow our past, or rather our unpleasant memories of the past, to determine who we are and how we perceive ourselves today.

When you allow the memory of a disappointment, a transgression against you or an act of cruelty to shape your perception of self, it can have a far-reaching impact on your own life and the lives of everyone around you. Fortunately, the healing of that pain can also have a profound effect on your life and the lives of those around you.

So, what is the secret for moving past those painful memories? It is simple. It is forgiveness.

> "*. . . . All you have right now are the memories of all*
> *those things . . . . And it's the memories you respond*
> *to now, not the past itself.*"
> —Serge Kahili King, Hawaiian shaman and author

The Power of Forgiveness

Let me share the story of a little girl whose life was forever changed when she began experiencing sexual molestation at the tender age of four. The abuse continued for more than three years. The offender told her not to tell anyone. Because it was an extended family member and because she did not want to embarrass him or the family, she kept silent. When she finally did say something to someone, actions were immediately taken to ensure her safety and security.

This little girl lived just above the poverty line and grew up to be an overachieving A-student—well-liked by her classmates and teachers. No one knew her dark secret, and no one knew that, in her mind, her self-worth was established during those years she was a victim.

When she was twelve years old, the offender passed away, and she thought she was "over it." However, those memories still came back to haunt her, and each time she felt the same loathing for her offender and for herself.

When she was sixteen and had grown to be a young woman, she learned about forgiveness. Not a fairy-tale forgiveness taught in school or church—rather, a deep, loving forgiveness that healed her deeply and changed the course of her life forever. Instead of continuing on a path of victimization, self-loathing and poverty, her life took a decidedly different direction. She became the first person in her family to go to college and soon after became a highly-paid executive. Eventually, she reconnected with her ancestral traditions to become a shaman healer and life coach.

You have probably figured out by now that I am that little girl. I am so honored and grateful to have gone through everything in my life, so I can help you live the life of your utmost possibility. Looking back on my life, I can say with absolute certainty that it changed dramatically after I forgave my abuser. The lock and chain that bound me to the belief that I was a victim were broken off forever, and my life has been abundantly blessed ever since.

True forgiveness is a powerful catalyst for change. I would argue it is *the* most powerful catalyst. It can shift the energy in a room, heal a relationship and change the direction of your life.

What Forgiveness Is Not

People sometimes resist forgiveness because they think that if they forgive, it will let that person *off the hook*. Nothing could be further from the truth. Here is what forgiveness is not.

- **Forgiveness is not exoneration.** Just because you forgive someone does not mean the person is pardoned. It does not mean the person should not be held accountable for his or her actions.

- **Forgiveness is not pretending it did not happen.** When you forgive a person, circumstance or situation, you are acknowledging that a transgression *did* occur, and you are taking action to release yourself from the power of that memory.

What Forgiveness Is

There are many schools of thought on what forgiveness is. As a shaman and a healer, this is what I teach.

- **Forgiveness is love.** In its purest intent, forgiveness is about love. It is the ability to love past a person's intentions, actions and beliefs. It is the ability to love them with all their faults, foibles and shortcomings. When you forgive, you experience *being in the present moment with joy* on an ongoing basis.

- **Forgiveness is empowering.** It is a part of tapping into your power. When you forgive, you release the power the memory has on your thoughts. This, in turn, is reflected in your actions and how you treat yourself and others.

- **Forgiveness is awakening.** When you forgive, you open your mind and spirit to your Higher Self. Your Higher Self is the part of you that instinctively knows what is in your best interest and can guide you to your ultimate freedom.

- **Forgiveness is releasing.** At the moment of true forgiveness, you release yourself from the chains that bind you to that memory. It is not that the memory is gone. It is that the memory no longer has the power to affect your thoughts, feelings and actions. You release the hold it had on you, and you are able to easily and freely let go of the pain.

- **Forgiveness is looking at a situation as an observer, not as a participant.** When you practice forgiveness, you are able to look at that person, circumstance or situation as an observer, not as a victim. You realize that the actions of the person or the set of actions that resulted in the circumstance or situation were simply that—actions that took place. It is like watching a television show or movie. You are not personally *in* that show or movie. You are merely *observing* what took place months or years ago on a set.

Hawaiian Approach to Forgiveness: *Ho'oponopono*

Ho'oponopono is an ancient approach to healing through forgiveness. Like other indigenous approaches, it may seem simplistic. However, do not underestimate the power of this process. The results are highly impactful and long lasting.

Ho'o is a Hawaiian prefix that means *to do*. *Pono* means *right, correct, good*. When you repeat the word *pono*, as in *ponopono*, it has double emphasis, which increases the importance. Therefore, *ho'oponopono* means *to correct* or *to make things truly right*. The powerful healing that comes from *ho'oponopono* allows you to quickly and easily move past the limitations that anger, resentment, disappointment and pain have on you and your life.

The *ho'oponopono* process uses the following elements.

• **Breathing.** Deep breathing oxygenates your cells, calms your energy and brings you to a place of relaxation. The Hawaiian word for breath is *Ha* and one technique is called *Ha Breathing*. In *Ha Breathing*, you inhale through your nose and exhale through your mouth. As you exhale, you softly say "haaaaaah." You inhale for two counts and exhale for four counts.

• *Aka* **Cords.** *Aka* cords are connections that are made all day, every day. Each time you think of someone or something, each time you look at someone or something, an *aka* connection is made. You can visualize *aka* cords as micro-thin cords that connect you with everyone and everything. During the *ho'oponopono* process, you will both connect and disconnect *aka* cords.

• **Visualization.** During the *ho'oponopono* process, you use visualization to bring in light and energy, create a healing circle, make *aka* connections, share *aloha*, cut the *aka* connections and fade the memory into the distance. Your visualization can be as bright and vivid or soft and muted as you choose to make it.

Ho'oponopono: **The Process**

It is important to remember that *ho'oponopono* happens in your heart and with *aloha*. You can use it on any area of your life, past or present. You may find that you need to go through the process more than once for some people, circumstances or situations. In one case, it took me more than six months and numerous *ho'oponopono* sessions to move past a situation. There were many layers to heal, and, eventually, I was free from the resentment and disappointment around it. So, do not give up!

With this in mind, follow the steps below and experience the magic of *ho'oponopono*.

- **Quiet space.** Find a quiet place with no distractions. This process may take you fifteen to twenty minutes at first. You will need a location where you can take the time you need for this quiet, reflective process.

- **Object of forgiveness.** Choose someone or something to forgive. This can be a person or an event.

- **Deep breathing.** Close your eyes, relax and begin deep breathing. Take at least sixteen to twenty deep breaths to bring you to a state of oxygenation and relaxation.

- **Visualization.** Begin to visualize. As you take your deep breaths, imagine a column of white light above your head. This divine healing light comes from Source, God, Spirit, Universe or whatever name you choose to use. As you breathe, allow that white light to enter the crown or top of your head and fill your body with its warm and powerful energy. As it fills your body from your crown to your toes and fingers, imagine it turning back onto itself, adding another layer of light and energy, all the way back up to your crown. There it erupts in a glorious waterfall of light, love and energy that both fills you up and surrounds you.

- **Healing circle.** As the light and energy continuously flow, imagine a large circle in front of you and just below you. This is your healing circle. You can create the circle in a meadow, a forest, a desert, on a beach, a mountain, a boat, a stage—anywhere you wish.

- *Aka* **connection.** Place the person or event in the center of your healing circle. Visualize the light that flows from above and through you passing through an *aka* cord to that person or event. Genuinely *feel* that light, love and energy going from you to the person or event in your circle. Look at the person and acknowledge that their actions were about *their* issues and not anything you did or did not do. Recognize that it was *their* illness, insecurity, past pain or ignorance.

- **Forgiveness.** With the *aka* cord connecting you with the person or event, slowly say the words, "I forgive you. Please forgive me. I release you." If you have anything else you want to say to the person, circumstance or situation, say it at this time.

- **Cut *aka* connection.** When you are ready, visualize a blade of bright light and lovingly cut through the *aka* cord. Watch as the healing energy goes back into you and back into that person or event. Witness the person or event in your healing circle fade farther and farther away, eventually disappearing altogether.

- **Deep breathing.** Take four deep breaths and open your eyes. Think of the person or event. Notice if any negative feelings still linger. If so, repeat the process as often as needed. When there are no negative feelings, you have experienced the full power of *aloha* and *ho'oponopono!*

I encourage you to implement the practice of *ho'oponopono* in your life. As you do, you will find that it becomes easier, and your ability to forgive and move on happens quickly. When you realize that you have the remarkable ability to release yourself from the hold that people and past events have on you, you will be changed. You have the power. You have the ability to create an amazing life!

YVONNE OHUMUKINI URNESS, CHSP
Healer, Coach, Speaker and
Founder of Hula for the Soul™

(408) 888-8967
yvonne@hulaforthesoul.com
www.hulaforthesoul.com

Yvonne is the founder of Hula for the Soul and a native Hawaiian shaman and healer who calls on the ancient rhythms of *hula* and the ancient wisdom of her ancestors to teach women how to experience fulfilled and purposeful lives.

A highly-paid corporate executive and communications consultant for global leaders including Nokia, Cisco and France Telecom, Yvonne eventually left her six-figure salary in corporate America to live her life purpose. She credits the Hawaiian principles of forgiveness, generosity and grace with helping her to achieve a healthy and vibrant life.

Yvonne's unique approach combining intuition, healing and business savvy have made her an in-demand expert who helps busy, successful women connect deeper with their passion, power and purpose. As a coach and speaker, she often incorporates *hula*, so participants experience how movement energizes the body and stimulates the mind. Yvonne is a Certified Hawaiian Shamanic Practitioner, *hula* instructor and dancer who has performed and competed on the mainland and in Hawai'i. She currently lives with her husband in Northern California.

Freeing the Body, Releasing the Mind, Moving into Action

Five Steps to Lifelong Health and Fitness

By Kym Belden, CHEK, USCF, ACE

Living the life of your dreams and having the power to change your body so it supports the fullness of life has as much to do with your physical function as your mental approach. Combine this with my *Five Moving into Action Steps,* and you have a sure combination for success—effective and fun to do as you free your body, release your mind and move yourself into action.

I am a fitness and sports performance expert and consultant. When explaining my career, I repeatedly hear, "I should exercise more," "I should join a gym," or "I should eat better and start an exercise program." Listening to this, my internal alarms go off. Yikes! With so many thoughts focused on what I should be doing, I would feel as if I was carrying a ball and chain strapped to my ankle, dreading what I *had* to do. This sounds like a sure sign of failure to me, which has driven me to create successful steps with real results that help change the body and the mind for a healthier, more vibrant life.

This chapter is dedicated to you. My wish is that you will be motivated to make a change *now* that will affect the rest of your life. Throughout my years of experience as a teacher, coach and consultant, I have discovered that what goes on in between the ears is just as important as what happens with the body. One hundred percent of my clients have a dream. Those who succeed in fulfilling their dreams and attaining their goals have done so by practicing these *Five Moving into Action Steps.*

Moving into Action Step #1: The Body

Oh, your beautiful body! Your body is a wonderful vessel of parts—joints, muscles, and so on—all working together, allowing you to perform the activities you enjoy. As with a car, it is important to keep your body's moving and stabilizing parts in good mechanical working order by using proper alignment. To move efficiently and injury free, I invite you to focus on these three important areas: your feet, your standing posture and your posture in motion.

Your feet. My client Cascadia is a hiker. She came to me because she loves to hike, yet her feet and knees gave her trouble one hour into her trek. Observing her standing and walking, it was evident to me why. The majority of her weight was shifted back in her heels.

As with Cascadia, your functional posture starts from the ground up. Just as the structure of a well-built house starts with a solid foundation, so does your anatomy. In fact, your feet are so important, how they support you determines your ability to acquire healthy results or acquire injury over time. It all begins at the feet and is specific to three points within the arch that I call the "tripod."

Action Exercise. Strip off your socks, grab a pen and use Diagram 1 on the following page as you go through these next steps. Consider your arch the bridge in your foot supporting the majority of your weight. Your tripod is located on the underneath side of your arch with two forward points and one aft.

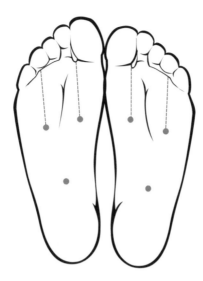

- On the bottom of your bare foot, draw a straight line down between your first two toes arriving at the top of your arch.

- Place a dot there.

- From your fourth toe, draw another straight line down until you arrive at the top of the arch.

- Place another dot there.

- The aft point is found at the lower part of your arch, in between the two upper points you just made.

- Standing up, try to distribute your weight evenly between these three locations. Remember, the front two points are able to handle more load than the single back point.

- From your collarbone, allow your body weight to shift forward, while hinging at the ankles until you feel balanced on your two forward points. Maintaining the balance on these forward points, gently add the one in back. Your job is to find equal balance between all three points of each foot.

- Lastly, ensure you are neither sticking your butt out, nor tucking it under.

Once you find your tripod's "sweet spot," you may feel like you are falling forward. This is okay, as your body simply needs to figure out its new position. Stand an additional three minutes to allow your mind and body time to adapt to the new function at your feet. If after these three minutes you still feel pitched forward, simply add on this next segment.

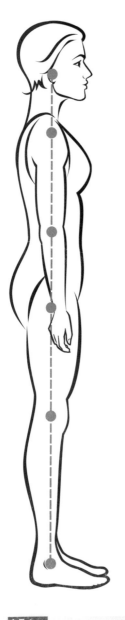

Your standing posture. Remember Cascadia's knees hurting? After identifying her lack of tripod support by shifting her weight back in her heels, she further compensated by pushing her hips forward of her midline. This caused her to round her upper torso backwards and jet her head forward. Ouch! Her imbalanced alignment was not allowing her joints and soft tissues to function in the manner to which they were designed. After an hour of hiking, her knees were screaming for her to stop. Let's make sure this does not happen to you.

Action exercise. Now that you are thinking about your foot support, let's take a look at what correct posture is. Looking at yourself in a mirror, stand sideways with your hands by your side. Using the diagram here, let's align the following anatomical structures from bottom to top, making subtle adjustments along the way.

- Your tripod

- The forward half of the bone on the outside of your ankle—the lateral malleolous

- The center of your knee joint

- The bone that sits like a bump on the outside of your upper thigh, before you reach the hip—the greater trochanter

- The top of your pelvis

- The elbow

- The shoulder

- The ear

The skeleton acts as *hardware,* and the soft tissues supporting and moving your skeleton act as *software.* With your posture aligned as in the previous diagram, your joints (hardware) experience balance and demand the appropriate musculature (software) to support and move your body in the way it is intended. When the hardware is aligned, the software can do its job.

What could poor posture be costing you? Like Cascadia, when your structure is out of alignment during movement, your musculature becomes imbalanced, creating unnecessary tension in areas of your body. With continued use, these stresses can result in inflammation and accelerated wear and tear on your affected joints, muscles, fascia, tendons and ligaments. Sadly, given enough stress, in time you will eventually see injury—the one thing that will stop you in your tracks from achieving your fitness goal. However, that is not going to be you.

Your posture in motion. Learning how to move in functional ways that are supportive to your body's structure is equal to having a golden key to success. You will have the power to resolve a biomechanical disorder or injury and the ability to gain health, strength and stamina while reaching all your physical goals.

Functional biomechanical posture (FBP) is a term that describes movement at its most efficient. It is your beautiful body aligned and supported during movement. FBP also assists your respiratory function and circulatory system, supports your internal organs and aids in your concentration and mental ability. Finding a coach to assist you in FBP during movement is key for finding your ideal alignment, preventing injury and successfully achieving physical success. It takes up to twenty-five percent *more* energy to function in a body out of FBP!

Moving into Action Step #2: The Vision

"If you aim at nothing, you'll hit it every time."
—Unknown

What do you want to attain from your fitness and gain in vitality? When you think of yourself as active and strong, what activity do you see yourself doing? Set some simple goals for yourself. Success coach, Brian Tracy states that writing down your goals will accelerate your chance of achieving them eighty percent of the time. In my experience, having goals is a powerful process and visualizing your goals adds to their success.

Professional and Olympic athletes utilize visualization techniques to help them perform at their best. If you watched the 2010 Winter Olympics, you may have seen images of many on the U.S. Ski Team® with their eyes closed, swaying as they visualized themselves going through their race in their minds before their start.

How it works. When you repeatedly think of an image, the reticular activating system (RAS) of your brain memorizes those mental images as something you want. RAS is the screening mechanism between your conscious and subconscious mind, and as a filter, it determines what information to call to your attention. Experts say that continual use of visualization causes the RAS to work by transferring your mental pictures to your subconscious, stimulating it to create solutions for acquiring the goals you want.

Visualizing yourself exactly how you want to be and feel can intentionally program your brain's RAS to deliver those same images to your conscious and subconscious mind. You will find yourself coming up with new ideas and begin acknowledging new sources of motivation as you take new steps in the directions of your goal.

In Jack Canfield's book, *The Success Principles,* published by HarperCollins in 2005, he explains that researchers at Harvard University discovered that students who practiced visualization before their activity performed with close to one-hundred percent precision. However, students who did not visualize in advance achieved only fifty-five percent accuracy.

> *"With mental rehearsal, minds and bodies become trained
> to actually perform the skill imagined."*
> —Elizabeth Quinn, American exercise physiologist

Now that your goals are known, it's time to create your vision. Right now, close your eyes. In your mind, imagine moving in any way that makes you feel good. More ideas will come as you continue to open this area of your mind. Keep visualizing yourself doing what it is you want to do and how you want to look and feel while doing it. Do not worry about anyone else, compare yourself to others or try to justify what you are doing. Keep it simple. Just focus on *you* and the results *you* want to achieve.

Moving into Action Step #3: The Coach

Expect success and plan to have a coach guide you through this process. We live action-packed days with commitments and endless forms of virtual communications that consume our time. It is easy to get distracted, bogged down or feel "I don't have time today to fulfill my goals." Coaches will guide you and hold you accountable, keep you on track when you detour and be your positive support when your vision gets out of focus. A coach will help you keep your eyes on the prize.

When looking for a fitness coach, ensure they are educated and skilled in:

• Biomechanics of the body *during* function

• Nutrition and sleep patterns

• Goal setting and achievement

• Program development, using entry through peak phases

• Recovery

• Positive reinforcement

• Accountability

• Trustworthiness

A sports medicine doctor or your physical therapist may be a great referral resource for someone skilled in your area.

Moving into Action Step #4: The Freedom

Another key to success comes in choosing recreational activities you *want* to do in environments you will enjoy. Success comes when allowing yourself the choice to move in ways that inspire you.

As a part of her fitness plan, my client Anita decided one evening that she would play soccer the following morning. Upon awakening she felt torn, realizing she wanted to swim instead. However, soccer was on her program and she had previously confirmed it with me. Now, she felt she *should* play soccer even though her heart was not in it.

Anita did not know the secret to fitness that will last a lifetime. The secret is this: *Simply do what you want by moving in the way you want to move!*

Be flexible with yourself and give yourself permission to change. Sound too simple? You would be amazed how many people prematurely fatigue in achieving their fitness goals by not allowing themselves to do what truly calls them. In this moment, please take time to sit back and relax. Take a few breaths in and out and then think about fun activities you would like to perform. Once you have come up with a few ideas, write down five ways of moving you would like to explore.

"Shoulding" on Yourself

The mind recognizes the word "should" as obligation, which is often followed by judgment. Use of the word "should" does not allow you the ability to choose. With enough "shoulding," you will feel frustrated, doubtful, disappointed and, eventually, unhappy. Ninety percent of my clients have been there. Have you?

This important issue is a critical reason why people prematurely quit their exercise programs, abandon the physical activities they could enjoy and give up entirely on their fitness aspirations. Staying stuck or attached to what you think you should do, have to do or need to do, as well as thinking about what worked for you in the past or what worked for somebody else, creates mental roadblocks. These roadblocks keep you from moving toward what you want. As a result, it disconnects you from your goal.

To get out of this pattern, simply replace the feeling of "should" with a choice–either *I will* or *I won't*.

You decide what you want. It is that straightforward. By having choices, you will be happier, and your brain will seek additional ways to motivate you and move you closer to your vision.

Try Something New

Your brain and body chemistry consistently change over time. Looking for the same results by repeating previous exercise regimes, diets and trends that worked for you in the past will not work for you today, even if you have the same goal in mind. Your ability to create success exists in every present moment, and your opportunity for success is right now! Design a new game plan you will presently enjoy. This will begin to stimulate your brain's pleasure center into motivating you to get started and to maintain your interest. Pick one activity from the five you wrote above and seize this opportunity. Take that one initial step. Get started.

Moving into Action Step #5: The Action

"If you don't make things happen, then things will happen to you."
—Robert Collier, American author

Energy creates energy. Taking action generates momentum. As in pedaling a bike, the first two to five strokes are the hardest to crank out. After a certain number of repetitions, the momentum you have created carries you more easily down the road. So does the momentum you generate in getting started toward achieving your fitness goals. Getting started may be a little difficult. However, as you move forward, the momentum you build will take you to your next step and build your motivation.

Acknowledging your actions is another key component in creating success. Do you know how most three-year-olds react when they do not receive positive acknowledgment after accomplishing what you have asked of them? The usual response is a tantrum with no interest in repeating the same endeavor. Adults are not much different.

We do not outgrow wanting to be appreciated and acknowledged, yet we simply mature to the point where we are able to appreciate and acknowledge our own accomplishments. As you aim towards success, take time to acknowledge and give daily appreciation for your accomplishments. You will generate momentum, and your brain will discover additional ways of keeping you motivated—a sure way to find your success.

Now, it is time to take action! Start by implementing the *Five Moving into Action Steps* that include:

• Body—for posture and efficiency of movement

• Vision—to clearly see you at your ultimate results

• Coach—for knowledge, support and motivation

• Freedom—to move in ways that free your body and release your mind

• Action—the first steps in creating momentum and energy to the final reward—the goal

There is no more planning or organizing needed. Just take one step into action. Pick up the phone, put on your shoes, make that appointment with your coach, get out of the house and take one step in whatever direction you need to create momentum. The smallest shift in focus toward your health and fitness done now can create amazing results in your future. If you were to take just five percent more responsibility for your physical goals, what would you do?

Remember, you are miraculous! You hold the power to decide what you want. You have all the potential to achieve your health and fitness goals within you. Use your power. Take action. Your time is *now!*

KYM BELDEN, CHEK, USCF, ACE
Physical Culture Consulting

*Becoming who you want to be,
enjoying the body you have*

(206) 779-4487
kym@kymbelden.com
www.kymbelden.com

K ym is a fitness and sports performance consultant, holistic lifestyle coach, USA Cycling™ coach and a success coach mentored by Jack Canfield. Since 1996, Kym has helped hundreds of individuals find their alignment, balance and strength to succeed in meeting their physical, mental, nutritional and emotional goals.

Kym is an accomplished expert in observing how bodies move, discovering their limitations and finding innovative ways for each individual to change their posture, function and vitality to be active in ways that bring joy to their lives. She is skilled in her application of holistic nutrition and takes pleasure in watching her client's health emerge into renewed levels of energy. Working with their mindset, she assists them to get out of their own limited way of thinking and coaches them into achieving the success they truly desire. She is passionate about sharing her knowledge with others in group settings and gives seminars throughout the United States and Canada.

A former professional dancer, Kym enjoys bicycle racing with her fabulous teammates. She currently resides in Seattle, Washington, and loves to spend her spare time with her guy, either on two wheels or in the country.

Using Rest as a Strategic Power Move

By Linda Michelle Trainer

merican poet Edgar A. Guest once said, "When care is pressing you down a bit, rest if you must but don't you quit." If the truth were told, how often have you wanted to do just that—*quit?* How often have you wanted to break away from your duties and responsibilities, from all of the demands for your time and attention—even from the passion it takes to see your dreams and goals fulfilled? Likely, you pushed yourself and ploughed ahead anyway. This can be a good thing at times. However, there is another important piece of the truth that *must* be told. If you do not take the time to step away from your responsibilities to rest, your body and your mind will suffer greatly.

Taking time out to rest is necessary for your overall health and wellness. However, how often do you allow yourself this precious time? Without rest, your body's ability to function as it is designed is threatened. When you do not get enough rest, your body becomes run down, your mind is stressed, and your spirit is weary. You may feel like a hamster on a wheel. Stress tears down, and rest builds up.

Just as our body automatically alerts us when it must be relieved of fluids or waste, our body also communicates its need for rest. Some signs are foggy brain, low energy and dark circles under the eyes.

How often do you put off or ignore these signs because you are too busy giving attention to other important matters? Your work ethic may be superior, and your accomplishments may be admirable; however, without a proper balance of work, recreation and rest applied to your daily regime, all of your commendable efforts can lead to despair.

"Fatigue is the best pillow."
—Benjamin Franklin, American statesman

Understanding Rest

The definition for rest I will be referring to in this chapter is from the *American Heritage Dictionary,* published in 1982 by Houghton Mifflin Company. It states that rest is "the act of ceasing from work, activity or motion; quiet, peace, ease, or refreshment resulting from sleep or the cessation of an activity." The bottom line is that the human body functions more efficiently after a time of rest. Positive, productive success in all you do can be optimized through the benefits of resting.

Dr. Matthew Edlund, in his book *The Power of Rest,* published by HarperOne in 2010, writes, "By using the body's unique power to restore and renew itself, you can look younger, lose weight more effectively and experience greater joy in your work and relationships."

If you were to take inventory of your own life, you would likely find examples of this to be true for you in one form or another. While Dr. Edlund agrees that pulling away and taking time to rest with all that you are faced with may feel like a *crazy* thought, his studies have proven it possible and productive. Human bodies are built to do things well at some times and to rest at other times.

Making Yourself a Priority

When traveling on an airplane as a passenger, you are instructed to put on your oxygen mask first before helping others. Your well-being is a prerequisite for the well-being of those around you. The same is true in your everyday life. Taking time to step aside and get still and quiet enables you to hear your inner wisdom. You will be better equipped to make quality decisions about your next course of action. Some of the solutions to the issues you face can be found by listening to that small, still inner voice. During a time of rest, you will be able to hear your thoughts. You can recognize your own voice, even if it has been muffled by the chaos around you.

When you neglect time to rest, you can become like a locomotive that is out of control, racing down railroad tracks at top-notch speed. The hectic pace of your life, filled with challenges and pressures—even those that are the result of something positive—can cause you to derail. Just as a locomotive that is running out of control has a danger indicator light flashing on the control panel, you have your own flashing indicators as well.

A safe, sure way to stop the train without destroying it is to pull back on the brakes with deliberate determination, power and force. Stop the train. Turn off the engine of your mind. Be still. Rest. By doing this, you are not abandoning your responsibilities. You are making space for wisdom, renewed power and strength to come forth. Yes, at times it can be difficult to make this shift. However, in order to clearly hear, you have to shut down the noise and be still.

Answer the following questions:

• What can I eliminate or cut back in my life?

• What truly matters most to me?

• What does rest look like to me?

• What do I love to do that is relaxing and enjoyable?

Once you answer these questions, you will have a clearer idea of the steps you need to take to welcome rest into your life in your own way.

Ways in Which the World Supports Us to Rest

There are many ways in which the world around us exemplifies and supports rest. Rest areas are provided for motorists along highways and expressways. Rest is mandatory for pilots, flight attendants and emergency response workers after working a set amount of hours. The rhythmic silence in music is called "rest." When I replace the ink cartridge on my printer, I am prompted before using it by a message that reads, "aligning cartridge, please wait."

The fresh perspective that follows a period of rest helps you realign your thoughts and emotions and enables you to remain undisturbed by setbacks. Your energy is renewed and fortified. From a place of rest, if you are knocked off of your feet, you can pick yourself up, dust yourself off and plant your feet deeper into the soil of your purpose. From the refreshing place of rest, you fortify your determination to go forth.

The *Time for You, Renewal Retreats* I conduct have proven to be an empowering source of healing and rest. The retreats are an intentional, purposed time away for personal reflection, pampering and encouragement. We incorporate a two-hour naptime on Saturday afternoon. Sleep is not forced, yet quiet time in a relaxed position is mandatory. The testimonies from the participants are always refreshing. Many share that they have not taken a nap since they were children. They say that they return home rejuvenated and revived.

Rest as a Personal Decision

"In the middle of difficulties lies opportunity."
—Albert Einstein, German physicist

In 2007, I spent thirteen days in a mental health facility after being misdiagnosed as having bi-polar symptoms. What I actually had was adrenal fatigue, also knows as adrenal exhaustion. The adrenals are two small glands that sit on top of your kidneys. Their job is to regulate your stress hormones, primarily adrenaline and cortisol. The adrenal glands give you increased focus and stamina to deal with sudden situations that require your full attention and effort. To cope with the stressors and strains on the body, your adrenal glands faithfully pump out extra energy to you. Adrenal fatigue occurs when the adrenals reach the point where they are barely functioning. Some of the symptoms appear as extreme fatigue, depression, frequent illnesses, hormone imbalance and the inability to cope with stressful situations when they arise.

To help me understand what was happening, my doctor used the analogy of my body being like a car that was empty of gasoline. She said that I was forcing it to move, pressing relentlessly on the accelerator and paying no attention to its needs. In my life, I was going full force, trying to tend to all the pressing needs around me. There was increased stress in my job and commute as a flight attendant, as well as a growing demand for services and training in my nonprofit organization. My husband was going through a major change in his career, and my father was diagnosed with terminal cancer. I was overwhelmed and stressed beyond the max! My body was depleted, and I did not know how to slow down.

The days in isolation in the hospital came as a blessing in disguise, and my life transitioned for the better. I experienced an awakening that could not have come to me in any other way. I ate three healthy meals each day. I spent at least thirty minutes outside in the sun daily and was in bed by nine o'clock every night. That alone was miraculous. I had not followed that kind of routine in years. Eventually, my body was able to rest, and my mind became sharper than ever. I gained valuable insight and understanding. For treatment, I was given a recommended diet to follow, a list of supplements to take and strict instructions to reduce my stress levels and implement rest into my daily regime.

After my return to work, several people, many with tears in their eyes, spoke of how they could personally relate to my story. It prompted several of them to visit their doctors to have their own testing done. I share these personal details with you in the hope that you will use it as a checklist to evaluate your life and make the changes that are necessary for your optimal well-being. With awareness and understanding comes power. Power is the ability or capacity to act or perform effectively.

The Benefits of Rest

Here are some clear, notable benefits of rest:

• Decreased cortisol levels, the hormone that increases in times of stress

• Decreased respiratory rates

- Decreased blood pressure

- Rejuvenation

- Physical and emotional well being

- Muscle healing

- Increased ability to concentrate

- Creativity enhancement

Rest can take the form of simply stilling your body and mind while remaining awake, or it can be a true falling asleep. Getting a full night's sleep, at least seven hours, can support you in feeling ready to take on the day's challenges. Sleep plays an important role in our immune functions, metabolism, memory and learning ability. When visiting other countries, I have observed different forms of rest, such as the *siesta* in Latin countries. A *siesta* is a one- to two-hour nap after the midday meal. Shops and businesses are closed during this period, so the workers can rest and refresh their energy.

Although your responsibilities in life may not allow for a one or two-hour nap every afternoon, a twenty-minute power nap can provide a fresh burst of new ideas and energy.

Break the Stress Before the Stress Breaks You

Plain and simply put, you must rest! A healthy mind and body are no accident. They come with conscious effort and focused choice. If you take care of your body and your mind by incorporating regular periods of rest, it will benefit you in ways that can reshape your world. Taking time to rest—even before you get tired—can fuel your brain and your body, adding quality to your life in every area.

In boxing matches, both fighters are required to stop fighting at certain points in the match and retreat to their respective corners.

In those few seconds of rest, each fighter is able to assess the damage, see his opponent, plan his next move and receive encouragement as his trainer tells him, "You can win this!"

It takes strength to sustain success. Biblical wisdom, 1 Peter 5:8, *The Bible, English Standard Version,* encourages us to be "sober and vigilant." Neither of these can be accomplished if your body and mind are exhausted. When you are weary, give yourself permission to rest. You must have strength to gain and sustain success in life. To R.E.S.T you must:

- **R**ecognize that you are not being lazy. A power nap will make you more productive and alert after you wake up.

- **E**mpty your mind. Thoughts, plans and worries can interfere with your ability to relax or fall asleep. If you need to, write down everything that is on your mind on a piece of paper. Put that paper aside, knowing that you can return to it later if you choose. This will free you to enter into relaxation.

- **S**leep. Give yourself permission to sleep or rest for approximately twenty minutes each day. If you are not sleepy, then simply sit still, perhaps read a book or listen to music. Ideally, do this at the same time each day. This will help you unplug from stress.

- **T**rust yourself. Trust that you can do this. You have what it takes. Your body knows what to do, and you can allow it to support you and let yourself fully rest.

> *"In quietness and in trust shall be your strength."*
> — Isaiah 30:15, *The Bible, English Standard Version*

Honor Yourself!

You possess the power. You are in control of your choices and decisions, your desires and actions. Determine your highest priority and your deepest joy and then make time for them. Change *is not* easy—it *is possible*. You have the power within you to take the necessary steps to see your desired change manifested in your life. Know that it is possible. Listen for the warning bells of stress and take the necessary time-out. You will benefit immensely from slowing down, pulling back and allowing yourself to receive the nourishment that comes with needed rest.

Do not miss out on your life because you are too exhausted to participate.

- Be proactive toward your health by communicating with your health care providers and doing your own follow-up research.

- Take daily time-outs to cultivate your creativity.

- Observe your thoughts and choose to give attention to what really matters.

- Work, play, rest, repeat. One without the other would be like three tires on a car.

Rest when you can because you must, and do not quit. Give your life your best shot and take care of yourself in the process. I have heard it said that when your body is ready to rest, it will enter that rest state with or without your permission. I invite you to give your body permission to rest *now*. Take encouragement when I say, "You can win!" Creating time for healthy rest in your life is the most strategic power move you will ever make.

LINDA MICHELLE TRAINER
Elegant Doves International, Inc.

The pain of understanding and healing is far less than the pain of denial and despair.

(770) 310-6434
lindamichelle@elegantdoves.org
www.elegantdoves.org

A possibility-thinker filled with a great passion for life, Linda Michelle is a flight attendant and the founder and director of Elegant Doves International, Inc. Through her company, she offers practical and effective strategies of hope and healing from the repercussions of childhood incest and abortion decisions made from a wounded spirit. Linda Michelle's personal and professional vision is to see women and teen girls healed from the emotional scars of their past, breaking generational cycles.

Linda Michelle is a certified discipleship counselor and is currently pursuing a degree in psychology with a focus in biblical counseling. Sharing the benefits of her experiences, studies and spiritual insights, she mentors women and teen girls from around the world. She is the author and producer of *Be IN Courage,* a CD series of inspirational messages of hope and encouragement. Her expertise includes appearances on television and radio and serving as a keynote speaker for women's conferences and retreats.

Linda Michelle's transparency and joyful attitude empowers women with courage and hope. Her sincere desire and dedication is to see women of all ages, nationalities and backgrounds healed and whole, moving from their pain to their purpose.

Discover Your Sacred Self and Eliminate Your Everyday Stress

By Madan Bali, PhD

Whether you are a successful entrepreneur, an active professional or a busy stay-at-home parent, you are likely to experience stress in one form or another. It is often when you are alone or in silence, faced with your own self, that your hidden fears or unresolved issues bubble to the surface. What is important to know is that these conscious or unconscious fears and issues are all being translated into your biology, creating toxins and stress hormones that accumulate in the body.

The good news is that the body has limitless technology within it. This technology is being orchestrated moment by moment to maintain and sustain the body in a state of inner balance. Infinite levels of activity are being processed simultaneously and spontaneously, silently and effortlessly, for renewal and rejuvenation. If our incredible technology were to function at its optimal level, it would be possible to encounter only overwhelming feelings of joy and peak experiences of wellness.

For this to happen, the deep healing capacity of the body needs to be restored. Healing takes place mostly during deep sleep when the mind is calm. This is the essence of yoga—the quieting of your mind, so your entire nervous system is calm. This optimizes your internal system of communication to help repair, replenish and regulate your biorhythms. Biorhythms are the inner cycles that affect your emotions, intellect and physiology by controlling things such as your memory, temperature, coordination, mood and metabolism. The constant chatter and busyness of your mind, coupled with continual stress, interferes with the body's natural ability to balance and heal itself.

The body's innate capacity is always there, dormant, waiting to be tapped into. Yoga, as a holistic approach, outlines the precise steps necessary to create health, happiness and wholeness. Yoga provides the tools and guidelines you need to help tame your mind, live more in the present moment and feel a sense of self-sufficiency and confidence in your ability to heal yourself. In short, yoga helps you lead a fulfilled life.

Our Current Predicament

As mentioned above, our bodies have an automated, computer-like technology within that works with unfaltering, mathematical precision to maintain a state of internal homeostasis—a state of perfect balance. If this is true, then why do millions of people suffer from a multitude of physical disorders, emotional pain and mental agony? In spite of our body and mind being so infinitely resourceful, why are so many people sick and unhappy?

Humanity is perhaps undergoing the most critical period in its evolutionary cycle. A sense of uncertainty, a lack of trust in others and ourselves, a polluted environment and political and economic instability are all contributing to an overload of stress and strain that may feel overwhelming. The body's innate adaptive response is, therefore, not able to function properly.

Currently, many people are dependent upon prescription drugs to help them. However, these drugs are not addressing the deeper problem. According to Ivan Illich in his book *Medical Nemesis,* published by Calders and Boyer in 1976, no matter how good the medication is, it is still interfering with the autonomy of the healing process.

We are spending millions of dollars on research to understand the measurable and visible aspects of the mind and body. However, the root or underlying cause of disease is in the mind. Unless we can weed out this cause—the negative emotions logged in our cellular memory such as fear, anxiety, worry and anger—our systems will continue to experience an excess of the fight or flight response. This response undermines the body's capacity to heal itself.

> *"Human unhappiness results from humanity's acceptance*
> *of the poorest conditions of our own minds.*
> *Through the practice of yoga, this condition can be overcome."*
> —Patanjali, Indian yoga master and writer

Yoga as a Holistic Solution

What is needed today is a holistic approach that integrates the body, mind and spirit, so we can discover our true nature and its infinite possibilities. At the level of the rational mind, we are too confined and limited in time and space. Conversely, at the level of the intuitive mind, our sense of self expands to experience the timeless, ageless and primordial source of infinite possibilities.

Yoga works on the physical body as well as on the emotional, mental and spiritual aspects of existence and helps harness the energy that is otherwise being dissipated through emotions. The underlying cause for our overloaded brains is our constant mental chatter. Our energy gets consumed too fast, too soon. Our brain and nervous system function like the roots of a plant. When the roots are not nourished and healthy, the plant cannot flourish. The same principle applies to our body.

There are eight limbs of yoga, developed centuries ago by the sages of India. The limbs are guidelines for making wise and clear choices in life and are primarily designed to help one rise above the normal human limitations. Ideally, they are practiced simultaneously to create a complete yoga experience. The eight limbs offer a practical methodology—a prescription for optimal healing and wellness. They help you discover your true nature and find your inner sanctuary of peace and love where your sacred self resides.

The eight limbs of the system can be broken down into three main groups—the ethical practices, the physical practices and the meditative practices.

Ethical Practices. This first group is made up of two limbs. These limbs are most often left out of Western yoga practice, thus contributing to the underlying cause for human suffering. They provide the very foundation for personal and social behavior, helping us make better choices that shape our destiny. Having refined habits such as these will ensure that you will have the inner strength and character to put into practice the other steps.

• *Yama. Yama* relates to social behavior and outlines activities that we should refrain from—for example, stealing and violence.

• *Niyama. Niyama* refers to personal observance and are behaviors to strive towards, such as purity, study and discipline.

Physical Practices. This group deals with the physical body through postures and breathing. In yoga, the body is viewed as the temple for the spirit. Therefore, caring for the body is an integral part of spiritual practices.

• *Asanas,* or postures, are now the main focus of yoga in the West. They were originally practiced in order to prepare the sages for deeper levels of meditation. *Asanas* help us access areas where there are hidden pockets of tension. Through gentle stretching, compression and muscle contraction, *asanas* help decongest deep tissues and allow for increased absorption and assimilation of the body's own medicinal needs. The body is so self-sufficient, it has the equivalent of a complete inner pharmacy.

• *Pranayama,* or breath control, is a primary focus of yoga. It is the prana or life force within us. The breath is our most precious source of fuel or energy. *Pranayama* exercises deal with controlling the breath, so it can be used to cleanse, energize, balance, relax or release emotions.

Meditative Practices. The next four limbs are closely linked—one moves imperceptibly from one limb to the next.

• *Pratyahara* means withdrawal of the mind from the senses and from the objects in the external world. The purpose of this is to experience the wholeness of the present moment.

• *Dharana* means concentration or holding the mind at one point with relaxed awareness. Its purpose is to tame the mind to stillness.

• *Dhayana* means meditation. This is when we come into direct contact with our Source—the Source of all creativity, intelligence, energy and love.

• *Samadhi* is higher levels of consciousness that lead to union with the divine. *Samadhi* leads to the ultimate experience of your true nature of *sat-chit-ananda,* which is a state of absolute awareness, bliss and freedom from human conditions. The realization of your true infinite nature is the culmination of the practice of these eight limbs.

"We are not human beings having a spiritual experience.
We are spiritual beings having a human experience."
—Teilhard de Chardin, French Jesuit priest, scientist and philosopher

The Bali Method™

My approach, called The Bali Method, is inspired by and has as its underpinnings the eight limbs of yoga as well as what I have experienced and observed during my forty years of teaching and practicing yoga therapy. My method is a therapeutic wellness system with a focus on leveraging the body's infinite intelligence and its infinite resourcefulness and capacity to mobilize itself. Regular practice of the method will help in promoting physical, emotional and mental strength and stamina. The method is now being clinically researched with cancer patients and is being offered at several hospitals.

In North America, yoga is often associated with a form of exercise that helps to build abs and "buns of steel." However, what is needed is to calm the mind and activate our guts. Our gut, or digestive system, has been clinically shown to be the second brain. It produces, independently of the higher brain, the same neuropeptides that the brain does. Neuropeptides are small molecules used by neurons to communicate with each other. Our gut needs to be healthy and decongested, along with all the other organs and glands, in order for the whole system to function at an optimal level.

The postures and breathing techniques I have chosen to focus on help to decongest the guts and increase circulation, which carries all the nutritional and medicinal requirements, to nourish the brain cells, tissues, vital organs and glands. They also help to tame the scattered mind that constantly drifts into the past or the future. That is where all your fears and anxieties come from. Whether they are conscious or subconscious, these thoughts are changing your biology from one moment to the next.

Since negative thoughts like fear, anger and anxiety have become part of our lifestyle, our bodies are often loaded with stress hormones and toxins that inhibit the body's own ability to heal itself. Yoga postures and breathing can dislodge these toxins. With practice, you can create a conscious shift and learn to suspend the mental chatter and create a single-pointed concentration that unites the body, breath and mind in the present moment where there is no stress. Only then can the wisdom of the body take over. Every detail for healing is taken care of silently and effortlessly. With consistent practice of The Bali Method of yoga, you can evolve into higher levels of awareness, improve your health and lead a life with less stress and more joy.

> *"Who looks outside, dreams; who looks inside, awakens."*
> —Carl Jung, Swiss psychiatrist and influential thinker

A Routine for Increased Wholeness, Wellness and Joy

Here are some general principles of The Bali Method to keep in mind as you practice.

• Begin and end each yoga session with a relaxation period of five to ten minutes. Relaxation is more important than the postures themselves. This is when the deep healing takes place.

• Hold the postures within your own limits and try to build the intensity of your practice over time. The greater the intensity of the postures, the greater the body's ability to tap into its inner reserves and the deeper the relaxation that follows.

- Relax between each posture and listen to your body. Focus your attention on the breath. Feel and cherish all the sensations that arise.

- One of the main premises of this method is to consciously focus on the transition between effort and effortlessness—to become aware of how the body feels during exertion and then observe closely the feeling of release and rest in between poses. Paying close attention to this transition helps to induce the relaxation response and shift you out of the fight or flight response into feelings of deep release. Through this conscious process, your mind and body and its cellular memory become reprogrammed to help with absorption and assimilation for optimal health.

The following routine of *asanas* and *pranayama* will bring about positive results when practiced twice daily—once in the morning and once in the evening. Results will increase over time, so patience and trust are essential.

Pre-posture relaxation. This relaxation, done for five to seven minutes, helps to shift your attention from your busy day to a quieter inner space. Lying on your back in a comfortable position, gently bring your attention to your breath. Allow your breath to continue its natural flow. Let yourself become a silent observer or witness to all that is going on in your body, without judging or trying to change any-thing. Your energy goes where you attention goes, so by keeping your attention focused inward, you are relaxing your body and increasing your energy reserves.

Postures. Follow The Bali Method *asanas* for optimal wellness for fifteen to twenty minutes. The *asana* routine can be found on http://yogabliss.ca/postures. The postures help to build core strength and stamina and dislodge accumulated stress hormones. While they bring about physiological benefits, they are also a way of calming the mind to help you conserve energy and hasten the healing process.

Breathing. An essential aspect of The Bali Method is a breathing exercise called *kapalabhati*. In Sanskrit, *kapala* means skull and *bhati* means to shine. Thus, *kapalabhati* nourishes the brain, the respiratory system and the nasal cavities. It also decongests the guts, massages inner organs and glands and boosts circulation to the cerebral spinal centers. This helps the brain to process information efficiently and hastens the body's ability to heal itself. Additionally, the vagus nerve is connected from the diaphragm to the heart chambers and helps to improve cardio output. This nerve continues to the mid-brain. It has been clinically shown that the body can produce its own anti-depressants and endorphins that produce a euphoric-like experience through vagus nerve stimulation, similar to what happens during *kapalabhati*. *Warning: If you have high blood pressure, you should avoid this exercise.*

Sit comfortably. Rest your hands on your knees with the thumb and index finger softly together, in what is known as *gyana mudra.* Close your eyes. Inhale normally and then exhale quickly and forcefully while sharply contracting the lower abdominal muscles, like when you cough. If you focus your attention on the rapid exhale, the inhale will happen automatically. This is a very potent exercise, so in the beginning, complete three cycles of ten to fifteen swift exhalations, then gradually increase up to twenty or thirty.

Deep relaxation. Again, lying on your back, bring your attention to your breath for five to ten minutes. Allow all your muscles to relax. Imagine all the benefits of your yoga practice now being translated into your physiology and your cellular memory being reprogrammed. Feel the shift towards effortlessness that induces feelings of comfort, peace and bliss. You may want to visualize a time in your life when you felt at your best. Imagine what you were doing at that time, how you were feeling and what you looked like. Allow these memories to enter your sacred space and feel the energy inside you, just like when you were in your best shape ever. Linger with these blissful feelings. Relaxation is not something that you do—it happens by you allowing it to happen. All you need to do is let go of all expectations that inhibit the process. During relaxation, you hasten your body's ability to mobilize itself and tap into its own innate healing powers to help regenerate and rejuvenate itself. Feelings of peace and serenity are the body's way of telling you that you are healing at a deep level. Enjoy the feelings!

The change you will experience from a regular practice is a shift from the head to the heart, from thinking to feeling, from your rational mind to your intuitive mind. All pain and suffering is experienced at the level of your rational mind. As you transcend the rational mind and get in touch with your sacred space, you will have the power to turn your fleeting moments of happiness into lasting feelings of peace and joy. Rather than trying to make this shift, I invite you to simply trust. Understanding and insights come in the silence of practicing yoga. Silence is the natural state of the mind—freedom comes when you dwell in the inner silence. Connecting with the Source through silence, the jigsaw puzzle is solved. The question *Who am I?* is answered when you realize you are one with the Source, one with the Universe. You are whole and perfect just as you are. Your sacred self is the Source, the co-creator, the center of the Universe and, in the infinity of your sacred self, is a knowingness that all is always well.

Madan Bali, PhD
Yoga therapist, Vendanta Scholar, Author
and International Speaker

*Turn your fleeting moments of happiness
into lasting peace, joy and bliss*

(514) 932-7971
info@yogabliss.ca
www.yogabliss.ca
www.drbali.ca

D r. Bali is the founder of Yoga Bliss, a research and training center based in Montreal, Canada, since 1969. Born in northern India, he developed an interest in a spiritual path from a young age. For more than forty years, Dr. Bali has successfully introduced yoga to several schools and colleges, as well as hospitals, corporations and community centers. He has developed yoga as a complementary form of therapy in treating psychosomatic disorders.

Dr. Bali is a living example of how to lead a healthy lifestyle. Nearing his nineties, he continues sharing the joy of yoga in his classes and international conferences. His work is also featured in several documentaries. Dr. Bali is a Vedanta scholar with a doctorate in complementary medicine and is one of the best sources of wisdom and knowledge about yoga, its philosophies and its applications for living a fuller life.

The Bali Method, used by hospitals and cancer foundations alike, is based on the principle that the wisdom of the body knows best. With its own pharmacy and finest automated technology, it allows one to tap into the body's infinite potential for health, happiness and wholeness.

Change Your Environment, Change Your Life

By Linda Lenore, FSM, CGBP, IAD

Change happens as long as you are alive! You are a work in progress, and you are never the same. You are constantly changing. As the Greek philosopher Heraclitus said, "You can't step into the same river twice."

You are like a river, flowing and changing as you wind around the bends in life. Sometimes, you tumble over the rocks in rapid, tumultuous, out-of-control movement. Sometimes, you come to an eddy, whirling slowly around and are able to view situations calmly from all perspectives.

We might be fortunate to have the river of life flow into a large open area, like a lake or pond, where we can settle into life, contemplating all that surrounds and enfolds us. At moments like this, where introspection occurs, dreams of a different life, a different way of "doing" life, or possibly even having more time to "be" with life can happen. We come to the conclusion that we want to initiate changes ourselves.

However, not all change is invited or planned. Sometimes, life situations happen unexpectedly—a sudden illness, death, job change, altered relationships or financial redirection. Instead of allowing ourselves to be a victim under these challenging circumstances, we can be proactive and move the condition toward a more favorable state through small, yet subtle, energy shifts in our homes.

Planned changes in life, like marriages, children, further educational endeavors, new living arrangements in another home or town, or new relationships can be more closely aligned to our preferred outcomes when we invoke action steps within our current living quarters. These actions can become part of sacred life passages through more directed or ritualized patterns of your own creation.

There is power in place. We can harness positive qualities that exist in our homes. If negative vibrations exist, we can alter them to generate positive, high-vitality qualities to produce powerful places for our lives. This chapter will give you ideas and tools for changing your environment to change your life.

Chi—The Vital Life-Force Energy

For several reasons, I use the analogy of water to express how the energy of our lives transitions. One reason is the various forms water can take. These forms give accurate expressions to how our lives move and change. Ideally, we would like things to "flow" smoothly.

A second reason is the power, sacredness and reverence associated with water. Water's powerful force can be destructive from hurricanes and tsunamis. We pray for rain during droughts. For relaxation, we use its restorative powers at the shoreline or spa.

Another reason for using the analogy of water is *feng shui*—the words literally mean "wind" and "water." This many-thousand-year-old art, science and philosophy addresses every aspect of our living environment, both inside and outside. It is designed to bring the best of all energy to the occupants of buildings. It is a tool we implement during times of change to achieve a desired outcome.

Have you contemplated the role water plays in your life? When thirsty, you want to drink it. When dirty, you want to cleanse yourself with it. You want it to grow plants. These examples change something that *was* into something that is *wanted*.

Feng shui considers water to be a form of *chi,* the life-force energy necessary for all things living. Water flows, helps create life, finds ways to move around obstacles and settles into the low flat areas, thus bringing life to them.

As one of my masters stated, "One-quarter inch of water grows grass, which attracts insects to eat it. Birds come to eat the insects. Animals come to eat the birds. Humans come to eat the animals. Water gives life to all."

When experiencing a change in your life, try to relate it to a form of water. This gives you clues to help you implement change in your environment—to support the change process while infusing vital life force energy, or *chi,* into your body and life.

For instance, if you feel blocked or stagnant, where do you have stuck *chi?* Is there clutter? Do you enter into your home faced with a wall that blocks your view of the rest of the building? If so, place a painting or picture of a landscape containing a depth—like a lake—in the foreground with mountains in the background.

If life seems to be roaring out of control, how might you arrange the furniture within a great room? Just like the riverbanks and rocks set boundaries for the water, thus forming a gentle current, could you create a pathway to an intimate seating area symbolic of guiding your life in a desired direction? This process reinforces daily activities, thus programming your subconscious. In this case, the pathway set by furniture signifies boundaries that lead to serenity.

The *Feng Shui* of Environments

For more than twenty-five years, I have been studying and utilizing *feng shui* principles in my life and the lives of my clients. I have found applying *feng shui* guidelines extremely beneficial in supporting my life and pursuing my dreams and desired outcomes, especially for unplanned situations when life *just happens.*

For instance, about fifteen years ago, shortly after my husband, Hilory, was diagnosed with throat cancer, I woke up in the middle of the night convinced I needed to move boxes from the hallway. I could not understand this need until I remembered that one of the schools of *feng shui* uses the analogy of our human body within our buildings. Briefly, this particular school states the foundation of a building is our feet, the studs within the walls are our bones, and the roof is our head and hair. This same school says the hallway is the throat. That meant these boxes were a foreign object, just like the tumor in Hilory's throat, blocking the flow of *chi.*

This situation, in which I felt I had no control over life circumstances, gave me an action step to change the energy of the house to support his well-being. It definitely changed my awareness of our home environment by directing my intention toward Hilory's healing.

Interestingly, there were three men in my life at that time with cancer of the mouth and throat. Two of them died. Hilory is alive, without having experienced any further issues with throat cancer. Who can say for certain what, if anything, moving boxes had to do with this desired outcome of health and life? It might not have had any influence, yet it might have improved the vibrational energy of the home enough to create a supportive, healing environment needed for long-term health.

Another example where I used *feng shui* to change my life also involved Hilory. Before I met him, I was terribly discouraged from having dated for years and not finding a suitable relationship. I decided to create an altar in my bedroom with objects that represented qualities I desired. I also conducted a ceremony in and around my home, acknowledging challenging areas of my environment, particularly the "missing relationships" areas. I did this by placing a rock in the location where the exterior walls would need to intersect in order to *fill in* the house to have relationships. I did this while invoking prayers of love, thus changing my thoughts and feelings about my home and life.

Within a week, Hilory came into my life. He is my soul mate. He possesses even more wonderful qualities than I had dreamed possible.

This is the power available to us when we include changes within our environment as part of the process to help with changes occurring in our life. The most powerful results occur when we think through the process to include thoughts, actions and words with feelings. We are empowering our body, mind and spirit to become actively involved in the change and to set the direction of the desired intention.

The Power of Place

Sometimes, when change is happening or needed, we change our environment by traveling to a different location. Vacations are a great way to get a new perspective on life by taking us out of our habitual daily patterns. We experience life in a different way. Organizations or businesses plan retreats and off-sites, literally taking employees away from their comfortable and predictable office to think-tank locations that stimulate brainstorming or teambuilding.

Have you ever returned from vacation or a business trip to realize your home needs major reorganizing or cleaning? Living in it day-to-day, it is difficult to see what it really looks like. Even more important than how it looks is how it feels. When you walk into your home, do you feel uplifted by its vibrancy? If not, you will want to make changes to your environment.

> *"If you want to find the secrets of the Universe,*
> *think in terms of energy, frequency and vibration."*
> —Nikola Tesla, Serbian inventor

Everything has a frequency and vibration since it is made of vibrating atoms. When items are not in harmony with each other in a space, it creates a discordant energy. Discordant energy makes us feel out-of-sorts, preventing us from thinking clearly or moving forward easily during times of change.

Sometimes, we vibrate with an object or place, feeling a resonance with it. We are attracted to it, or it to us. Some places just *feel* like home. We resonate with an area, thus wanting to revisit it again.

The qualities expressed by a place may be the qualities we need, or qualities we consciously or unconsciously strive to have in our lives. A trip to the pyramids connects us to ancient civilizations. Trips to sacred sites, like Stonehenge, activate our awareness of sacred symbols. Traveling to healing centers, both natural and man-made, change negative health experiences into powerful, positive healings.

The Power of Symbols

Mankind has used and understood the power of symbols throughout history. Swiss psychiatrist, Carl Gustav Jung wrote the book *Man and His Symbols,* published in 1969 by Doubleday & Company, Inc., to discuss the meaning and use of symbols throughout our existence.

He wrote, "A word or an image is symbolic when it implies something more than its obvious and immediate meaning. It has a wider 'unconscious' aspect that is never precisely defined or fully explained. Nor can one hope to define or explain it. As the mind explores the symbol, it is led to ideas that lie beyond the grasp of reason."

You can use the power of symbols to shape your life. Symbols can invoke sacredness, healing, vitality, luck, beauty, joyfulness, child-like wonder, adventurous travels, closer family ties, loving partnerships, financial serenity and so on.

Here are some known examples:

- A *mezuzah* on the doorpost is deemed a protector for Jewish households. It invokes sacredness in the home.

- In the Asian culture, guardian lions or dogs by the front door symbolize protection of the home, as well as greeting visitors.

- Even numbers play a symbolic role. Placing objects in sets of three symbolizes a sacred trinity in many religions. Two other numbers are one and nine. Multiples of these numbers are also considered powerful.

- Native Americans honor the energies of animals, often creating carvings from wood and stone. They place these carvings in strategic areas within their home—sometimes to honor their ancestors or for protection.

Using the power of symbols from different cultures, especially from your own heritage, can help you define your deepest wishes for your home. Discovering what to use and where to put it is part of the process of supporting the changes you are experiencing or need to initiate.

The Power of Water

A universal symbol we will use in several areas is water. Water is a symbol of health, wealth, prosperity and vitality. If you do not have water in one of its many forms, you may miss an opportunity for the riches of life. Water is symbolic of the feminine and emotions. When change is happening, and you need the emotional or nurturing qualities of the feminine, water in one of its many forms is a perfect solution.

Water placed outside the front of the home brings prosperity to the occupants. Water features near the center of the inside part of the home give vitality to the area, bringing with it health. Having water features in the back left corner of a building symbolizes enough wealth within the household to allow a circulation of money in the form of giving back to society.

Actual water, verses a picture, is always lovely to have, as it brings a sense of serenity to most areas. In the event physical water is not a viable solution, perhaps due to danger for children or animals, the use of water pictures can be used. These pictures need to be vibrant with lots of water—not just a little creek, but a river and not a small pond, but a serene lake enveloped by a large mountain range. The lake symbolizes your need for emotional support as you are being held, nestled in the strength of solid mountains.

The Power Points of the Home

Every location within the home has its own energy and many symbolic meanings. There are colors, objects and elements associated with each area. There are parts of the body, like ears and head. For instance, the kitchen relates to health and the heart. Kitchen elements are fire and water. If near the center of the house, you will want to add earth and the color yellow as they represent the element and color for the center of the building.

Bedrooms are the inner sanctum for our soul, the area of love and romance. Softer pastels usually work well, yet sometimes we need a splash of red to bring a fiery spark to relationships or dark blue to water down aggression. The room in the back left corner of a house controls finances and gold accents are good here. The back right room represents relationship and pink or peach does well here. You can visit my website to get a chart of how to orient your house and determine what each room relates to.

Power Processes for Change

Here are *feng shui* suggestions to support change in your life. When considering the areas of your home, look at it from your perspective as you enter the front door and face the interior of the house.

- To initiate changes in your life, move 27 items that have not been moved in a year.

- To promote health, place a healthy plant in the center of the home or bring yellow into the area.

- To support job and career issues, place pictures of you doing things you love by your front door.

- To improve study habits and encourage further education, display books within view of the front door, especially on the left side as you enter.

- To generate closer family ties, display photos on the middle left-hand side of the home.

- To stimulate prosperity consciousness, gather money in a jar or bank in the back left corner of your home. Wealth and security reside here.

- To bring vitality to your reputation, brighten the middle back section of your home with lamps, candles or display colors of red and orange.

- To entice loving partnerships and intimate relationships, place objects in pairs or pictures of couples in the back right corner of the home.

- To connect to your creativity and playfulness, exhibit your handiwork and pictures of children in the middle right section of the home.

- To encourage connections to mentors or to travel, place a mirror in the front right area of the home. Display travel posters and books here as well.

Powerful Pieces Put Together

When change happens in our lives, whether through exterior circumstances or interior motives, we have the ability to make simple, yet powerful, changes to our homes to aid the process. Our homes are safe havens in the storms of life.

Here is how to put the pieces together.

- Examine the change in your life. How do you feel about this change? If you hold negative feelings, find positive ones.

- Is there a place in your home that is a power point as described in the previous section? If so, will the suggestion associated with it work for you? If not, do something symbolic to you in that area to create a positive feeling in that part of your life.

- What is the *chi* of this change? Remember, *chi* is the life-force energy vibration in and around us. Are things moving too fast, are they out of control, or do you feel stuck? What can you do symbolically to change the frequency and nature of the situation?

- Can you use water in some form to alter the energy of the location? Remember, water has many qualities to draw on during times of change.

- Create a ritual or ceremony while you are changing your environment. Get emotionally involved with the process positively by allowing yourself to energetically feel some positive emotions like love, gratitude, passion, excitement, joy, hope, satisfaction and enthusiasm.

Your thoughts and intentions become integral pieces you use when changing your environment to initiate and support changes in your life. Remember, everything in the universe has a frequency and vibration that attracts like energy to it. If the change you want or are experiencing is not expressed in your home, you will not attract the desired outcome to you.

Your home is the heart of your life. Create the desired energy in your home, and you will change your life equally.

LINDA LENORE, FSM, CGBP, IAD
Green Chi Designs

Creating healthy, high-vitality homes with a heart

(650) 368-5532
Linda@GreenChiDesigns.com
www.GreenChiDesigns.com
www.LindaLenore.com

More than 25 years ago, when Linda heard that her home contributed to her son's death, her *feng shui* journey began. Ten years later, she discovered a different home was adding to her illnesses. She and her husband personally remodeled it using green and sustainable building principles.

Linda is a *feng shui* master, certified green building professional and vital office/vital home consultant. She is the only person in North America who holds all these credentials. Through her company, Green Chi Designs, she is known for creating corporate and home environments that both stimulate success and soothe the soul. Her clients include Adobe Systems®, The Half Moon Bay Ritz-Carlton Spa®, TiVo® and numerous media personalities.

Linda was selected as an American Society of Interior Designers 2008 Distinguished Speaker, was interviewed for a European documentary and was a University of California faculty member. She has appeared on radio and national television. Known as *The Healing Decorator,* Linda's writings and presentations inspire audiences through design, ancient wisdoms and story. You can view her Hallmark® Channel segment *Building Your Emotional Home* by visiting her website.

Gift of Change
Consciously Creating the Change You Want
By Summer Simonton

We humans are the only living creatures we know of who have been given the gift of being able to deliberately and consciously create what we want and change who we are and how we live our lives. Unfortunately, most of us seem to have forgotten that. In this chapter, you will be given tools to help you remember this gift.

In order to comfortably move from where you are to where you want to be, you must embrace change. Most of us want more, yet we do not want to make the changes necessary to get it. Often, even the mention of the word *change* makes many feel uncomfortable.

Your very thoughts, beliefs and imaginings have created your life the way it is now—where you are. If you really want more—to get where you want to be—you have to change the way you think and behave.

"Change has a considerable psychological impact on the human mind. To the fearful it is threatening because it means that things may get worse. To the hopeful it is encouraging because things may get better. To the confident it is inspiring because the challenge exists to make things better."
—Whitney Young, Jr., American mediator

When you think about changing, what comes to mind? Are you excited about it, or do you live in fear about what might happen? Do you start imagining the worst outcome, or do you imagine how much better things could be? Would you be happy if five years went by, and you were still the same—making the same amount of money, working in the same job, having the same kind of relationships, having the same body weight or size? Even though the answer is likely *No*, most of us still avoid making the change necessary to make our lives different.

What makes change uncomfortable are the daily habits you have created, which mostly serve to make you *comfortable*. Stepping outside that comfort zone causes stress and fear. The reptilian part of your brain, which is responsible for protecting you, views anything unknown as a possible danger.

The beliefs you have about yourself, others and the world become habitual ways of thinking over time. For example, it is common to talk about what you don't want rather than what you do want. Since the mind thinks in imagery and does not have an image for "don't," you are actually imagining, thus creating whatever follows the word "don't." For example, your mind translates, "Don't forget your keys" as "Forget your keys." It can only create an image of you forgetting them. "Don't be late" is translated as "Be late."

When my clients start to tell me what they don't want, I help them refocus by asking them what they *do* want. The more you get comfortable thinking and talking about what you do want, the easier it is to bring it about and the more comfortable you will be with the change when it happens. Mentally rehearsing what you want not only brings it about, but it also helps you feel comfortable with the change.

> *"Imagination is everything.*
> *It is the preview to life's coming attractions."*
> —Albert Einstein, German physicist

Using Your Imagination

To start living your life the way you want it to be, you must use your imagination, words, thoughts and feelings to mentally rehearse what you want as if it has already happened.

Most of your beliefs were formed in childhood. As a child, you lived in a wondrous state of imagination where you believed everything was possible.

This belief started changing as you began to observe your environment and you bought into the belief systems of those around you. This helped create new habits, which continued on into your adult life.

Have you ever challenged your beliefs? Ever wondered if they are true or if they only appear to be true because you believe them? Have you ever asked yourself what would happen if you choose a different belief?

Here is an exercise to help you become more aware of your limiting beliefs.

1. Make a list of your limiting beliefs. Think of different areas of your life, such as money, relationships, success, your body or size, what you think you are capable of or not capable of, and anything else that might be keeping you from leading a more fulfilling life. Observe what you say after the phrase *I am a person who* . . . You might need to ask friends to point out what you say after that phrase because you are rarely aware of what you are saying or thinking.

2. Challenge your limiting beliefs. Ask yourself if your beliefs are true. Are they what you have told yourself for so long that they have become "true" in your own mind? Perhaps you bought into other people's beliefs based on your perception of them or what you were

told. What if these beliefs about you and your abilities are not true? What if you are just one changed belief away from living your dream?

A client of mine started gaining weight when she was forty. As she started challenging her beliefs, she remembered that when she was young, she was the only thin person in her family. Her family told her that when she turned forty, she would gain weight. She had completely forgotten this until she made her list of limiting beliefs. She then realized she must have believed it because at age forty, she started gaining weight. She easily lost the pounds after challenging and changing that belief.

An attorney who attended one of my workshops often said, "I am a struggling attorney, and I have terrible clients who often don't pay their bills." After she became aware of what she was saying, she changed her beliefs about being a struggling attorney and not making money. That year, she tripled her income, started her own law firm and imagined the type of clients she wanted. She has continued to be successful and is enjoying her work. Without changing her old beliefs, she would probably still be wondering how she was going to pay the rent.

Another client who was a single mother with three children realized she believed that no man would be interested in having a relationship with a woman with three children. I asked her if it was possible that a man who could not have children would want them. She agreed that this was possible. She changed her belief and was open to the idea of what was possible. She started visualizing such a man. Within a month, she met a wonderful man who was thrilled that she had children because he could not have them and always wanted them.

3. Create a new belief system. Choose what you want to experience and thought you could not have. Ask yourself:

- What if my beliefs are not true?

- What if I really am capable of being successful, in love, prosperous, healthy, the size I want to be, dancing and creative?

- What if the beliefs about me and what I have been telling myself are not true?

- What will happen if by changing my beliefs, my abilities and possibilities change?

Practicing in My Own Life

When I came into a greater understanding of the power of changing my beliefs, I heard myself say that I was not a creative person. I would not even take an art class because I knew I would fail. After all, my brother was the artist in the family. I used to say that I could not even draw stick figures to look like anything recognizable. When I heard myself say this, I asked, "What if this is not true? What if I really am creative and really am an artist? Would changing my belief about that possibly change my abilities?"

I went home and took out a piece of paper and a photo of my friend. I said to myself, "I am an artist, and I can draw my friend from this photo." I received some guidance that sounded like a voice telling me to relax, forget the lines and draw the light and the dark. Since I had not had training on how to draw, I thought that was a little odd, and then I heard it again. This time, I paid attention and started looking only at the light and dark. It was so much fun and so easy! When I finished, my drawing looked just like my friend!

In that moment, I knew what I had believed was not true and I became an artist. I made large collage wall hangings, sculpted, painted, drew, made masks, produced a short film, started writing poetry and pursued many other creative endeavors. These were all things I did not believe I could do before I challenged my beliefs.

After that, I knew I could do anything creative that I wanted to do. Changing that belief opened my life up to a completely new world and a new me.

From that experience, I asked myself what other things I had believed that might not be true. I realized that I told myself I was not athletic, so I challenged that as well. I started telling myself, *I am athletic and can do whatever I decide I want to do.* To test my new belief, I went snow skiing with a group of friends Snow skiing was something that had been a very humiliating experience for me in the past. I would spend most of my time falling down the slopes instead of skiing down the slopes. However, this time, I sat and watched people skiing for a while and told myself I can do that. I took a lesson and did well. I had fun, too! After the lesson, my close friend took me to the intermediate slopes, and I was hooked on skiing. All I did was change my belief about who I thought I was and what I could do.

In one of my workshops, a new real estate agent said that she had not made a sale or had a listing in her first six months as a real estate agent. I asked her what beliefs she was telling herself about that. She said she had the belief that her past profession as a nurse was about helping people and her current profession was not. After I suggested that real estate was all about helping people make their dreams come true, and how they needed an agent to offer them support and expertise, she was excited to take on that belief. Within two weeks, she put four houses in escrow and went on to be a successful agent. This all came about from changing her belief.

FutureSpeaking

If you are ready to let yourself start easily making some changes so you can start living your dreams, you will enjoy this easy and powerful technique that I developed thirty years ago, called *FutureSpeaking*.

FutureSpeaking is speaking about your vision, goal or dream with the same emotion and enthusiasm as if it has already happened. It is speaking in such a way that you convince yourself and anyone listening that it really has happened. You are letting it be known and accepted as a current reality. You use only positive words that are the same vibration or frequency of what it is that you desire.

Every word has its own frequency or vibration. Radio stations, television stations, cell phones, the Internet and so on all have a frequency you tune into by clicking or turning a dial. The same is true with your words, thoughts and feelings. When you use positive words that are the same frequency as your dreams and goals, you begin tuning into and attracting them, as if you were a giant magnet.

Use words that create a positive image of what you *do* want, and it will empower you. Here are some examples:

Instead of saying:	Say:
I am debt free	I am financially abundant
I have lost weight	I am now a toned, size ____
I do not want client problems	I am enjoying fun, qualified clients
I do not want relationship problems	I have loving, positive relationships

Next, write what you want to be, do or have as if it has already happened. Make sure every word is a positive frequency of what you want. Write a paragraph as if you are writing to a friend and telling them what you have manifested in your life. Read this several times a day, saying it to yourself or to someone close to you.

In case this sounds too simple or you are skeptical, another real estate agent announced in our first class that she was skeptical and was only

there because her colleague said she was negative. She said she had very little business because the economy was against her.

Months after the workshop, she called me and was filled with excitement. She told me that since she took my workshop, she closed four houses. The following year she reported closing twelve houses. She shared that her change in beliefs affected her whole life, including her family and children.

Are you willing to challenge some of your beliefs and open yourself up to new possibilities in different areas of your life? What would you like to experience that you have told yourself you cannot do or be? What if you are only one belief away from your dreams?

The most important question to ask yourself is, *If not now, when?* The time is now. The world needs your dreams to be manifested!

Summer Simonton
Speaker, Workshop Leader, Coach and Author

Empowering people to live their dreams

(415) 690-6996
www.FutureSpeaking.com
·summer@FutureSpeaking.com

Born into an Air Force family, Summer moved often and learned early the importance of embracing change. When she discovered the spiritual laws for achieving success from her *t'ai chi* teacher, her life changed dramatically. She quit smoking, lost thirty-five pounds and kept it off. She also became a successful entrepreneur and doubled her sales. She knew that she needed to teach this information, and she developed her own technique called *FutureSpeaking*.

To learn more about the power of the mind, beliefs and emotions, she attended the California Institute of Clinical Hypnosis, receiving a certification as a master hypnotist. She also received a certificate to teach *t'ai chi chih*.

Summer is considered a pioneer, teaching mental and spiritual skills for success, laws of attraction and guided imagery for achieving one's dreams. She has taught workshops to the general public, small businesses, real estate businesses and large corporations. She has been a keynote speaker for many associations and organizations and has appeared on local radio and television. Summer is a spiritual coach who has a gift for bringing out the best in people.

MORE **POWER** to *Change*

Now that you have learned about the power to change and have a variety of tips, techniques and strategies, the next step is to take action. Get started applying what you have learned in the pages of this book.

We want you to know that we are here to help you meet your professional and personal objectives. Below is a list of where we are geographically located. Regardless of where our companies are located, many of us provide a variety of services over the phone or through webinars, and we welcome the opportunity to travel to your location.

You can find out more about each of us by reading our bios at the end of our chapters or by visiting our websites listed on the next pages. When you are ready for one-on-one consulting or group training from any of the co-authors in this book, we are available! If you call us and let us know you have read our book, we will provide you with a free phone consultation to determine your needs and how we can best serve you.

United States

California

Alletta Bayer, LMFT, CDC, CHAAT	www.allettabayer.com
Beverly Lenz, RN, MS	www.beliefchangesystems.com
Linda Lenore, FSM, CGBP, IAD	www.LindaLenore.com
Lynn Kwitt RMT, CCA, CWC	www.thejoyofessentialoils.com
Pat Gayman, DC	www.capacitycoach.com
Summer Simonton	www.FutureSpeaking.com
Tammikka Chambers	www.TLChambersEmpowers.com
Yvonne Ohumukini Urness, CHSP	www.hulaforthesoul.com

Georgia

Linda Michelle Trainer	www.elegantdoves.org

Nevada

Annalysse Gilbert	www.drive-to-thrive.com

Oregon

Debra Liddell, CDC, CFH, CNH	www.theherbalnutritionist.com

Texas

Byron Ingraham	www.byroningraham.com

Washington

Brett Dupree, CPC	www.joyousexpansion.com
Kym Belden, CHEK, USCF, ACE	www.kymbelden.com

Canada

Alberta
Carol Connick, MD   www.SOULutionsCoaching.com
Janet Wiszowaty   www.familyconnekt.com

British Columbia
Ed Dowling, MscD   www.universallaws.co

Quebec
Jackie Roberge   www.cancershift.com
Madan Bali, PhD   www.yogabliss.ca
       www.drbali.ca

THRIVE Publishing develops books for experts who want to
share their knowledge with more and more people. We provide
our co-authors with a proven system, professional guidance and
support, producing quality, multi-author, how-to books that uplift
and enhance the personal and professional lives of
the people they serve.

We know that getting a book written and published is a huge
undertaking. To make that process as easy as possible, we have
an experienced team with the resources and know-how to put a
quality, informative book in the hands of our co-authors quickly
and affordably. Our co-authors are proud to be included in
THRIVE Publishing books because these publications enhance
their business missions, give them a professional outreach tool
and enable them to communicate essential information
to a wider audience.

You can find out more about our upcoming book projects at
www.thrivebooks.com

Also from
THRIVE Publishing™

For more information
on this book, visit:
www.getorganizedtodaybook.com

For more information
on this book, visit:
www.incrediblelifebook.com

Also from
THRIVE Publishing™

For more information
on this book, visit:
www.directsellingpower.com

For more information
on this book, visit:
www.momentrepreneurbook.com

Also from
THRIVE Publishing™

For more information
on this book, visit:
www.inspiredstylebook.com

For more information
on this book, visit:
www.mystylemywaybook.com

Also from
THRIVE Publishing™

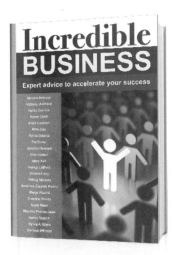

For more information
on this book, visit:
www.incrediblebusinessbook.com

For more information
on this book, visit:
www.connectionscountbook.com